I0122642

BACKCOUNTRY
EXCURSIONS

Other books by Walt McLaughlin:

Campfire Philosophy
Fragments from a Field Journal

The Great Wild Silence
Ruminations and Excursions in the Adirondacks

A Reluctant Pantheism
Discovering the Divine in Nature

Cultivating the Wildness Within

The Impossible Cosmos
A Year of Amateur Astronomy and Big Questions

The Unexpected Trail
Taking on the 100 Mile Wilderness

Forest under my Fingernails
Reflections and Encounters on the Long Trail

The Allure of Deep Woods
Backpacking the Northville-Placid Trail

Arguing with the Wind
A Journey into the Alaskan Wilderness

Loon Wisdom
Sounding the Depths of Wildness

Nature and Existence

Worldly Matters
Essays and Short Narratives

A Hungry Happiness

BACKCOUNTRY EXCURSIONS

Venturing into the Wild Regions of the Northeast

by

Walt McLaughlin

Wood Thrush Books

Second Edition

Copyright c. 2005, 2020 by Walt McLaughlin
All rights reserved.

Published by Wood Thrush Books
27 Maple Grove Estates
Swanton, Vermont 05488

ISBN 978-1-7345175-2-1

Acknowledgements

"Tracks Across the Forest Floor" was first published as a slender, self-published paperback (Wood Thrush Books, 1990), which has been out of print for decades.

"Snowshoeing in the High Peaks" appeared in the Adirondack Mountain Club publication, *Adirondac,* in 1997.

An excerpt from "Following Thoreau to Katahdin" was printed in the journal, *Heron Dance,* in 1998.

"Natural Causes" was reprinted in *Heron Dance* in 2001, after it had been published as a Cedar Tick Chapbook (Timberline Press, 2000).

"Natural Causes" has also been reprinted in *Loon Wisdom: Sounding the Depths of Wildness* (Wood Thrush Books, 2014). "Snowshoeing in the High Peaks" and "Pilgrimage to Lost Pond" have been reprinted in *The Great Wild Silence: Ruminations and Excursions in the Adirondacks* (Wood Thrush Books, 2018).

Contents

Preface

In the spring of 1990, Odyssey Press printed up 329 copies of "Tracks Across the Forest Floor" as a slender, sage green paperback. My life as an outdoor/nature writer effectively began with that. I had been writing fiction, poetry and essays since 1977 but didn't really find my voice until I wrote this piece. After spending five days alone in the Breadloaf Wilderness in the spring of 1988, I told my wife Judy that I wanted to recount the experience as accurately as possible. She thought that was a good idea so I set to work on the project later that year. Self-publishing the short narrative once it was finished seemed like the best way to assure the integrity of the piece.

By 2005, "Tracks" had been out of print over a decade. I had published two book-length narratives by then – one about hiking Vermont's Long Trail and another about my brief sojourn in the Alaskan bush – and thought a collection of shorter pieces would complement them nicely. With that in mind, I published "Tracks" along with five other hiking narratives as *Backcountry Excursions*. Sales were rather lackluster until a bookshop in New York City picked up the book in 2011. A year and a half later, that one shop had sold off all but half a dozen copies. I was happy about that. But with such a limited market, I couldn't justify reprinting this book. That is, not until now.

Thirty years have gone by since "Tracks" first reached print. To celebrate the anniversary, I am kicking out this new edition of *Backcountry Excursions* print-on-demand in order to keep the book in circulation indefinitely. Along with "Tracks," the narratives "Following Thoreau to Katahdin" and "Chili Dogs on Mount Washington" have no permanent home. And while "Natural Causes" and the other two pieces have been reprinted elsewhere, it feels right to keep all six of these early hiking narratives together. If nothing else, they provide a clear picture of my evolution as a woods wanderer.

This collection finishes appropriately with "Pilgrimage to Lost Pond." Even though "Pilgrimage" is based upon a hike I took back in 2002, it pretty much sums up who/what I still am. Fresh from yet another solo excursion into the Adirondacks this week, I feel the same connectedness to the wild now that I felt then. And my worldview remains pretty much the same. With over a dozen nature-related books in print, I have become the man I aspired to be during that first trip into West Canada Lakes Wilderness: a creature of the forest and philosopher of wildness. What a long journey it has been since the Breadloaf Wilderness outing back in '88! With much more to come I hope. I feel quite fortunate to have access to the wild regions here in the Northeast, and will continue venturing into them, pondering wildness and writing about it for as long as I can.

– Walt McLaughlin
July 2020

BACKCOUNTRY EXCURSIONS

TRACKS ACROSS
THE FOREST FLOOR

1

A mile-wide grin breaks across my face as I lean back in my chair behind the counter of the bookstore and begin daydreaming about mountain brooks, early spring flowers and footpaths winding through the forest. Tuesday evening, the middle of May. I've just called Mr. Niles. When he said he would take the Saturday morning shift, I thanked him a half dozen times, then quickly hung up before he changed his mind. The best thing about running your own business is not being answerable to anyone; the worst thing about it is trying to arrange time off. Usually my friends are pretty good about watching the store for me whenever I need to get away, but sometimes I can't fill a time slot to save my life. For two days I've been scrambling to find someone to babysit the store this coming Saturday morning. When Mr. Niles said he would do it, I became one happy camper. Now there is nothing standing between me and the trailhead but a little preparation and a long wait.

Wednesday morning early, I start getting ready for my five-day solo backpacking trip. I dump all my equipment, along with some clothes and a few personal items, into a huge pile in the middle of the living room. Grey light filters through the window bringing to mind a previous venture into the woods alone. Last October, I was caught in a freak winter storm and some of my equipment was badly damaged. When I got home, I took my gear to the attic and there it remained throughout the winter – dirty, neglected and unrepaired.

I check everything very carefully. My rubberized rain suit is shot – a recently acquired army surplus poncho will have to take its place. The tarp needs some patches here and there; the stitches in the seams of my backpack need reinforcing; my knife needs sharpening; and the crotch of my favorite hike pants needs to be sewn up. I put together a list of odds and ends to pick up at the store when I go shopping for food: extra band-aids, more matches, candles, and freezer bags. Midmorning, I walk away from the mess, going to my bookstore to pay any bills that I can't put off another week.

Wednesday evening. I begin the long but pleasant task of packing. I place selected pieces of equipment in a nice, neat row after cleaning and repairing them. Judy – my lover, housemate and best friend – sits on the couch watching me with a curious combination of admiration and bemused disbelief. She has observed this process before, but has not yet grown accustomed to it. I check and double check everything against a master list, then check it again. How ironic that a carefree walk through the woods should begin with such thorough preparation. In my defense, I can only say this: what is left behind must be done without, and having or not having an item can sometimes be the difference between a pleasant trip and a miserable one. There are a few things, like an extra box of waterproof matches wrapped in plastic, for instance, which could save my life someday. Oh sure, it takes a lot of time and effort to prepare for every contingency, but essential items are rarely expensive and usually take up little room in the backpack.

With Zen-like calm, I organize my gear. Anticipating the forest, I have learned over the years to discard the hurried, frantic headset of the city – as much of it as possible, as soon as possible – before starting a trip. My well-being depends upon it.

After sorting out my gear, I place food, clothing and anything else I wish to remain dry into plastic bags. This time of year, I can expect my pack to get wet at least once. One good rain soaks everything unprotected.

The faint scent of the woods arises from my backpack. So easy to imagine myself on the trail already. What have I forgotten? Ah, toilet paper, of course. I remove some from the roll, fold it, put it in a baggie, then stash it in the first aid kit (of all places). Emerging from the deep recesses of my memory comes the sound of the brook. Mustn't forget the bait on the bottom shelf of the refrigerator.

The final stage. The actual packing never takes long. I could put it off until tomorrow morning, but no, might as well do it now. Into the backpack it all goes: first the bag of extra clothes, then tarp, groundcloth, a water bottle, mess kit, food and miscellany. The first aid kit always goes on top. One side pocket holds the poncho; the other holds a second water bottle. Resting upon the chair are the clothes I'll wear tomorrow along with a few important items: pocket knife, hunting knife, matches, compass, map and wallet containing my name, phone number and address in case of emergency. Thanks to Judy, I now possess bungee cords which I use to attach sleeping bag, foam pad and collapsible fishing pole to the outside of my backpack. And there you have it. All ready to go.

I hoist the load to my shoulders to see how it feels and to make certain that the weight is evenly distributed. And it is. Forty-five pounds, I estimate. Quite manageable. I set it down, study my topographical map for the umpteenth time, then sigh heavily. It is getting late and I need a good night's sleep.

My cousin Bill has promised to pick me up tomorrow afternoon and take me to the mountains. I will spend tomorrow morning tying up loose ends at the shop, puttering about, twiddling my thumbs. I only have to wait now, to kill time, to pretend that I am patient. Eighteen hours to trailhead and counting...

One last phone call to the National Weather Service: chance of rain Thursday; dry Friday; chance of rain over the weekend. No word on Monday yet. Temps ranging between the 40s and the 70s they say, but a good bit colder in the mountains, no doubt. No major storms predicted, but you never know. I hope for fair weather, but will settle for overcast skies and a little drizzle. Any kind of weather will do, actually, as long as I can get into the woods for a few days.

2

Just being in the forest is its own reward. The best reason to head for the hills is for the sheer pleasure of it. I'm well aware of the obvious benefits of outdoor recreation, but I still harbor a few ulterior motives as I wait for the departure hour to roll around.

All winter long I troubled myself with a host of unanswerable questions, most of them a variation of the same theme: considering the nature of humanity, is there any legitimate basis for hope? In other words, will we ever be able to substantially improve our lot in this world, above and beyond the mere acquisition of material goods? Heavy stuff, very heavy stuff indeed, even for a brooder like myself who can't get his fill of that philosophical mishmash. But what can I say? Such things concern me, especially in January.

The cold season had been particularly long, or so it seemed. Winter lingered well into April, as it often does here in northern Vermont. I would have been a lot better off, no doubt, had I chosen a somewhat more cheerful matter to ponder through those long dark nights and short days, but I didn't. So now here I am, still in the belly of the beast, even in the month of May, even after the trilliums have flowered and the buds on trees have opened, even as I prepare for a trip into the woods. And that, I suppose, is why I am taking this trip in the first place.

Now obviously, one isn't going to solve the world's problems during a five-day trek through the woods. Even in my somewhat bent frame of mind, I am aware of this. All I can expect is a bit of temporary relief and, if I am lucky, perhaps enough recharging of the ol' spiritual batteries to keep me going for another year, despite what I think of the human condition. I have learned one important lesson this past winter: some dragons are just too big to slay. So now my only hope is to retreat to a little higher ground where I can reacquaint myself with myself, maybe discover some way to cope with it all, then get on with the business of living. It's a simple scenario: me as the sick man; the woods as the cure. I'm a little world-weary, that's all. A little time in the woods will set me straight, at least for a while. Perhaps some day, after selling the shop, I'll give that unwieldy question the treatment it deserves, but right now my spiritual energy is tapped. It's time to seek out the friendlier, more pleasant side of reality.

You have to be a little crazy to hike alone into the woods – I won't deny it. A jaunt through the forest is precarious enough when you travel with a companion. To go it alone is sheer foolishness. What risks does the solitary hiker take? Calculate the dangers inherent to backpacking, then multiply by ten. Who will go for help if I twist an ankle or fracture a leg? Forest rangers and hiking clubs try to discourage people from hiking alone and rightly so. A solitary hiker is much like a trapeze artist working without a net. It's just not smart, but there are a few madmen like myself who can't muster enough common sense to resist the temptation.

Alone in the forest, I feel so much more alive, so much more a part of nature that I believe the greater risk is warranted. Unless you are lucky enough to have a hiking companion who is incredibly sensitive, who can give you the space you need when you need it, you won't be able to simulate the solitary wilderness experience. When alone, one simply hears more, sees more and feels more, without the easy distraction of another person ten yards away. Besides, it takes a while for the wild to work its way into your system. An hour sitting alone in the woods before linking up with a companion for lunch isn't going to do it. It takes several days for that civilized veneer to wear away.

Alone in the forest, I've no one to impress, no one to bullshit except myself and after a while that gets old. Now I'm not saying that I can't maintain my illusions about the world while solo hiking through the woods – one can nurture one's illusions indefinitely. But when I hunger for a glimpse of truth, when I have a strong enough desire to cut through all the nonsense, especially my own, I go spend some time by myself in the woods. There is something about being human that makes it extremely difficult for us to be ourselves as long as someone else is nearby.

If the forest isn't real, then what is? If you can't find God in the wilderness, then where can you find him? Words like "god," "reality," "truth," and "nature" are all pretty meaningless when disentangled from each other. They all refer to the same basic phenomenon – whatever it is. Do away with one of those words and you might as well do away with them all. As some people have.

As for me, I like my illusions as much as the next guy, but there's a limit to how much of it I can stand. Eventually, it gets to the point where I have to feel the soil between my toes and splash spring water on my face in order to regain a sense of perspective. So I head for the hills, to be alone for a few days, to reacquaint myself with What-is. After a long winter of dark thoughts, it's the only thing left for me to do. By early spring, all other options have been exhausted.

3

Thursday afternoon. A steady rain is falling as my cousin Bill and I leave Burlington in his pickup truck. We drive south on Hinesburg Road. As we pass through Lincoln less than an hour later, the rain tapers off to a light drizzle. The pavement ends shortly thereafter. The dirt road to the trailhead winds through open fields and into the woods, following the New Haven River back to its source. Bill's fishing pole is in the back of the truck along with all my gear. Bill and I are both avid fishermen. We have decided to take advantage of the situation and probe the headwaters of the New Haven for brook trout before I hike alone up the trail.

Bill parks his truck a quarter of a mile shy of the trailhead – about as far as he can drive it down the muddy two-track access road, riddled with puddles. Stepping out of the truck, we hear the low roar of the river not far away. I work my collapsible pole loose from the rest of my gear, then extend it. The air, much cooler and cleaner than back in the city, smells of spring flowers and raw earth. Trilliums cover the forest floor and wood anemone blooms in thick white patches. We walk down the nearby path toward the steady rush of water.

We creep upstream, Bill on one bank and me on the other, taking turns casting our lines into promising pools and riffles. The rain has ceased now and the mosquitoes are in abundance – many freshly hatched today. We bear their assaults stoically as we fish, waving them away from our faces with a twitch of the wrist. The brook trout are biting but they are pretty small so we throw most of them back. We are far upstream – way beyond the point where brown and rainbow trout thrive, beyond the point where anyone can seriously refer to this stream as a river. Even though it is swollen from the downpour, we are able to cross back and forth over the brook without difficulty, stepping on stones to keep our feet from getting wet.

After fishing the stream a couple hours, we have nothing to brag about, but we have enjoyed ourselves all the same, crossing lines and grinning stupidly more often than speaking to each other. The sun slips behind the trees. I tell Bill that I have to be going. We quit the river and walk back to the truck. Bill has kept two fish. So have I. He lets me take them all so that I'll have enough for a decent meal this evening. Four thin trout, six to eight inches long, are just barely worth the trouble it takes to cook them. I thank him for the fish, thank him for the ride, then shoulder my pack. Bill smiles, wishes me a good trip, then drives away. And that is the last I see of anyone for a while.

Hiking up the Cooley Glen Trail, I listen to droplets fall through the tree branches, bouncing off leaves. The occasional chirp of a bird in the distance is the only other sound I hear. I want to put at least two miles of trail between me and the trailhead before twilight fades into darkness. That will take about an hour, I figure. Maybe less. There is still plenty of light. The leather straps of the grey, canvas, Norwegian pack on my back creak in cadence with my footfalls. I move quickly along the trail, maybe too quickly, missing most of the scenery. Small yellow and white flowers glow in the semi-darkness on each side of the trail. Fluorescent red efts crawl slowly across the trail in front of me, endangering themselves. I cut my pace as I step carefully around them. By the dim light seeping through the forest, I can just barely see their snake-like bodies among the rocks.

What's that? A chorus of a thousand spring peepers echoes through the forest. Their rapid, high-pitch croaking grows louder as I slip quietly through the woods, but they fall silent the moment I show myself on the edge of a clearing. For a short while, I search the small wetland hoping to catch a glimpse of one of those frogs as it leaps towards the water. I see only ripples on the water's surface, slowly expanding in rings. Darkness is closing in rapidly now, so I keep moving.

About fifteen minutes later, I notice that the path beneath me looks more like a freshly cut logging road than a hiking trail. When did I last see a trail marker? It's too dark to see them, anyway. I check my compass: thirty degrees off, at least. Not good. Something is wrong. It suddenly occurs to me how easily I could have strayed from the trail back at that clearing. Too late to do anything about it now. There's only a trace of light left in the sky. It's time to make camp.

I find a nice, flat piece of relatively dry ground near a small brook. By the time I have set up my tarp, any semblance of light is long gone. Down by the brook, I clean the fish and gather firewood by flashlight, muttering curses at myself for being such a tenderfoot. Not three hours in the woods and how many mistakes have I made already? Some woodsman. Between gulps of water and handfuls of gorp – mostly peanuts mixed with a few raisins and M&Ms – I break sticks about the thickness of my thumb and place them next to a hastily constructed fire circle. Then I make a small tipi out of tiny twigs and start a fire.

"Hoo-hoo-hoo-hoo-hoooo!"

I grab my flashlight, jump up, then shine the beam of light into the trees behind me. The sound of flapping wings pierces the air, then silence reigns again. In the distance, a little later, that hooting again – it's a great horned owl. I can hear him but I can't see him. Wants the fish, no doubt. Four brook trout lie in a nice, neat row on a plastic bag, next to the fire just now beginning to glow. Too bad he flew away. I would have shared my dinner with him.

I cut a switch from a nearby shrub, whittle the end to a point, then skewer one of the fish – first through the mouth, then into the tail. I cook the fish until its eyes are white, then devour it as I squat near the fire. I skewer a second and so on until all that's left of the day's catch is a small pile of fish bones. A carrot and another handful of gorp – so much for dinner. The fire quickly dies down to smoldering embers. The wood is wet and burns poorly, putting out more smoke than heat. It's not worth the effort it would take to boil water for tea. I'm kind of tired, anyway. After hanging the food bag from a nearby tree, I crawl into my sleeping bag underneath the tarp.

Next to the tent pole supporting a corner of the tarp, I push a candle halfway into the ground. By candlelight, I look over my topographical map. My exact position remains a mystery to me, even after studying the map a long, long while. I'm somewhere in the Green Mountain National Forest, a couple miles from the nearest improved road. Will have to get my bearings in the morning. Not a good way to begin a trip.

A twig snaps nearby and out comes my flashlight again. Its beam catches a pair of tiny eyes that quickly disappear in the underbrush. A field mouse intruding into my camp, most likely. Or am I the intruder? What business do I have being here, anyway? First night in the woods, I can't help but feel like an outsider, like maybe I'm out of my element, like maybe I should be back in town, in my nice, warm, dry bed with Judy. Lying under a tarp in the middle of the woods, alone, surrounded by nocturnal animals – I'm not quite comfortable here.

I slowly dose off to the soothing murmur of water breaking over rocks. After a while, it sounds like so many wood elves talking and laughing in the distance. Are they talking about me? I have heard them many, many times before, on previous nights alone in the woods. It's just my imagination, of course. But even after all these years, I still wonder…

4

By the light of morning, it is painfully clear to me that I am not even close to the Cooley Glen Trail. As I munch a handful of gorp, I walk over to a nearby clearing with map and compass in hand. By comparing compass bearings to distant landmarks, I determine my position – roughly a quarter mile from where I want to be. I've made a big mistake, but it's nothing a half-hour hike cross-country can't correct. The distinct depression in the treetops below and to the southeast indicates the brook where I will find the desired trail. While cursing myself for being so careless the evening before, I break camp. Dark grey clouds approach rapidly from the west. Even though the tarp is already wet from a midnight downpour, most of my gear is still dry. In order for it to stay that way, I have to pack up everything before it rains again.

Not too much later, I shoulder my pack and follow a south-southeast bearing towards the valley. I expect a shower any minute now, so I'm wearing my poncho. Dropping into a small ravine, I fight through some dense underbrush. Other than that, it's a pleasant hike through the woods, dodging trilliums. I find the trail without too much difficulty and follow it as it turns slowly to the east. Happy to be back on track again, a smile breaks across my face. A light rain falls, then quickly ends – just enough moisture to bring out the forest's wealth of color on this otherwise dismal grey day. The bright green vegetation; the chalk-white paper birches against the grey-brown background of other trees; the dark green moss on slate-colored rocks; the burnt-orange tint of dead leaves and pine needles; the chocolate-brown hue of the path I follow – my eyes greedily consume this visual feast, garnished with delicate yellow, white and purple violets. Thank god for rain!

Crossing the brook, I come upon a sign informing me that I am now entering the Breadloaf Wilderness. It is difficult to convey how I feel at this moment. The word "elation" comes to mind but hardly captures the mood. For the next few days, I'm more likely to see wild animals than my fellow man, and my ears are now safe from the noise of motorized vehicles.

As the trail ascends, spring retreats behind me. I hike back into time. The season is a week further along in Burlington than at the trailhead. At fifteen hundred feet, there is easily two weeks difference. The canopy overhead grows thinner as I make my way slowly up the side of the mountain. Here the birches, maples and poplars are just beginning to show their foliage, while back in Burlington they have fully leafed-out. Trilliums are still abundant, but wood anemone is conspicuously absent now, and the yellow lilies just beginning to open up near trailhead are not inclined to do so at this elevation. Underneath the trees, hobblebush blossoms – its clusters of white flowers appear to be everywhere. As I stop to take a gorp break next to a feeder stream, I catch the scent of Dutchman's breeches. They are in full bloom here, but they are just about gone in Burlington. At two thousand feet, there is easily three weeks difference. At this rate, I'll be standing in snow by the end of the day.

A hawk circles overhead, seeking its prey. Its silhouette stands out clearly against the light grey sky. Circling, dipping, circling – it glides with incredible ease through the air. As I watch it longingly, I daydream about flying... then I notice the erratic chirping of birds nearby. I look over to see a huge nest in a tree a bit to the south of me. The hawk's offspring? I sit still for a long while, waiting for the hawk to fly to that nest. No such luck. It glides in leisurely circles, aware of my presence, no doubt. When the chirping stops, the whole forest seems to fall silent. No wind, no rain, only that incessant dripping of water through tree branches and the low roar of the brook crashing over rocks in the ravine below.

First wood anemone, purple trilliums and lilies; now violets, painted trilliums and spring beauties – not to mention the countless other flowers I can't identify. It's a garden growing wild in all directions, as far as the eye can see. Although uncultivated, it's as lovely as any garden can be. What's the difference between a wildflower and a weed? Only our attitude towards it. When we are not so busy trying to make something else of the world, we can plainly see how beautiful it is already. Sitting in the middle of the forest, I can't help but wonder why we find it so difficult to leave things alone – not all things all the time, just some things sometimes. The forest in all its disarray is just fine the way it is.

Eventually, I resume my hike up the mountain. Between twenty-five hundred and three thousand feet, the forest undergoes a dramatic transformation: broad-leafed trees become few and far between; conifers become much more numerous. I hike up the steep rocky trail at a steady pace, stopping frequently to catch my breath. Before long, I stand in the heart of the boreal forest. There is an occasional yellow birch here and there, but mostly balsam firs and red spruce trees close in around me. The mist hanging in them thickens into a dense fog as the cloud ceiling overhead lowers itself upon me. This evergreen world – most of Europe and North America as it was long ago – takes me by surprise. The smell of pine fills the air. Lichen and moss are abundant now, much greener and in thicker mats. Fungus grows wherever it can affix itself. A thick layer of pine needles covers the narrowing trail.

A flock of blue jays escorts me during the final leg of my ascent. They fly from branch to branch, chattering excitedly. I am panting now, sweating heavily, straining a bit under the weight of my pack, but unwilling to stop because I know I am close to the end of my day's journey. Not too far ahead is the Cooley Glen Shelter, in the saddle between Mt. Cleveland and Mt. Grant.

Finally, I come to a junction with the Long Trail, which runs along the spine of the Green Mountains north-to-south. A minute later, I am standing in front of the shelter. With the sun obscured from view, I can only guess the time of day: noon, perhaps early afternoon. There are several hours of good light left if I want to continue, but no, I am finished hiking for the day. The shelter will be my home until tomorrow. I look forward to spending the rest of the afternoon wandering about with no load on my shoulders. I take off my backpack and breathe easy.

5

The Cooley Glen Shelter resembles a three-sided cabin sitting on a platform two feet above the ground. It is deep enough to accommodate a tall person, and wide enough to comfortably sleep four people shoulder-to-shoulder, perhaps six in a pinch. Being slightly under average height, I can stand up inside it, but have to be careful not to bump my head on the beams that support the roof. Directly in front of the shelter are a picnic table and a huge fire circle. The ground immediately surrounding the fire circle is bare, compacted soil – dark brown mud mixed with the charred remains of many fires. Not exactly pristine. It's a high-use area, to say the least.

Looking around, it occurs to me that I shouldn't be here. Each step upon the ground surrounding the shelter, or upon the heavily eroded trail nearby, only makes things worse. Oh sure, I'll be bushwhacking off-trail down the mountain tomorrow, but still I feel like I shouldn't be here. I wonder what this area will look like ten years from now. My fellow backpackers and I are loving the forest to death – certain parts of it, anyway. In the spring, the trails are wet and muddy and very easily damaged by footfalls. I promise myself that in the future I'll restrict my early-season trips to the lower elevations, and stay off the hiking trails until June. That'll lessen the impact I make, anyway.

I toss my foam pad and sleeping bag in the corner of the shelter, leaving ample room for anyone who might come along. I hang my wet clothes from nails protruding from the walls of the shelter. After changing into dry clothes, I feast on cheese, pepperoni, cookies, crackers and a little gorp. How nice to be warm, dry and have a full belly once again.

Clouds roll into the trees, creating a dense fog. My nose starts running. I sniffle. Tree pollen? Fungus spores? Mold? Against my better judgment, I pop an antihistamine. Sitting cross-legged in the shelter with my eyelids growing heavy, I fight off drowsiness. The fog seeps into the deep recesses of my brain. I listen to the wind blowing far away to the north, then to the lonely cry of a solitary chickadee, then to the sound of my own light breathing. Stillness. No wind, no rain. Deafening silence in the middle of the day. Head in the clouds now. To stay warm, I crawl into my sleeping bag. Soon I slip into a deep, deep sleep...

The rain comes down in sheets, waking me from my midday nap. The patter of raindrops hitting the roof resounds through the forest. An intricate chain of puddles crisscrosses the ground in front of the shelter. Although protected from the downpour, my clothes haven't dried out at all. Either I didn't sleep that long or the air is simply too saturated with moisture for anything to dry. Oh well. I doctor a small blister and some hot spots on my feet as I watch the rain fall steadily. Once it has tapered off to a light drizzle, I put on my cold, wet boots and go for a short walk.

In the ravine not too far behind the shelter, I find what I believe is the source of the Stetson Brook.

Weather permitting, I will follow it down the side of the mountain tomorrow, into the drainage basin below. The sides of the ravine look steep from this vantage point. There are still patches of snow on its shaded, northern slope. Rough going, no doubt, but nothing I can't handle if I go slow enough. I return to camp, collecting fiddleheads along the way. A real treat: a fresh, green vegetable for dinner!

A strange, muted squeak emerges from a rotten log near the shelter. Obviously a rodent of some sort. It falls silent as I draw near. I listen carefully but nothing breaks the eerie silence. Even the chickadees in the nearby trees are quiet as they flit from tree limb to tree limb.

After collecting branches from fallen trees a good distance away, I return to the shelter with an armload of wet, green sticks covered with moss, fungus and lichen. Even after stripping away the bark, I have my doubts as to how well my pathetic pile of wood will burn. To make matters worse, there is very little kindling available. The handful of twigs I scrape together is meager to say the least. Couldn't be harder looking for firewood in a swamp.

Confident that my fire-starting skills will save the day, I wad up a couple sheets of blank paper torn from my journal. I then make a rather heroic attempt to build a fire. A bit of a flame, then smoke, no good. Try again. The mere hint of combustion, more smoke, same thing. Determined to get a good fire going so that I can boil water for tea, I keep at it, starting from scratch a half dozen times. An hour or so later, I have a charred mess of twigs and sticks and no patience left.

Retreating to the shelter where I have fashioned a nest out of my sleeping bag, I sit down and brood. Inconceivable as it is to me, I simply cannot start a fire. How many times have I started fires in the rain? What's a little dampness? Will simply have to try again later.

With both bottles empty, I go over to the nearby stream to replenish my water supply. I add an iodine tablet to each bottle of water to kill the bacteria in it. And what will I do about giardia – that bane of backpackers, that tiny water-borne parasite which only a thorough boiling can eliminate? Chances are, I tell myself, this water is safe. I am near the source of this high-mountain stream and there is no sign of beaver in the immediate neighborhood. But, on the other hand, there have been other hikers here and hikers do more to spread giardia than beavers do. How I wish I had a filter! After the tablets have a chance to do their stuff, I drink the water and hope for the best. The taste of iodine lingers in my mouth – anything but pleasant. I long for a cup of hot tea.

Afternoon late or early evening – it doesn't matter. A feeling of timelessness prevails. With nothing to do and few distractions, I sit for a long, long while, just staring into the clouds. The faint outlines of spruces and firs emerge like phantoms from the fog, then fade away. My thoughts, or what pass as such, are but random images loosely linked together. The lingering effect of that antihistamine takes its toll on me. A vague feeling of desolation and loneliness creeps into my head. To escape it, I slip into a netherworld of fantasies as I gaze with unfocused eyes into the formless grey-white curtain, which surrounds the shelter. After what could be either minutes or hours, the grey light grows dim. The sun sets somewhere beyond the clouds, upon a horizon I can only imagine. I go to sleep but not without resistance, certain in some inexplicable way that there is still something left for me to do today. I close my eyes and the evergreens shrouded in mist haunt my dreams.

6

Saturday morning, third day out. The sun burns through the clouds as it rises into the sky. Temps in the fifties. No fog. A good day to travel.

For breakfast, I eat corn flakes soaked in condensed milk, which I have extracted with some difficulty from a can. Then I drink as much iodine-treated water as I can stand, in anticipation of a hard hike. After orienting the map to true north, I study it carefully. Although I will be following the brook downhill all the way, I determine a compass bearing just to be on the safe side: east-northeast. Two-miles-plus – a short enough hike, but over extremely rugged terrain and with no trail to follow. It will be an adventure.

Less than an hour after crawling from bed, I have my things packed and am ready to go. I start down the steep slope behind the shelter, following a small game trail running parallel to the ravine. Thirteen hundred feet below, somewhere near the middle of the Stetson Brook drainage basin, is the end of a dirt road. I will eat lunch and make camp there later on today. A simple plan. All I have to do is stay on my feet for the next three hours and not twist an ankle.

The first half a mile is extremely steep. It's good that I'm negotiating it now since I tend to very cautious at the beginning of a descent, slacking off towards the end. I follow the easiest route down the side of the mountain, straying from the brook at times but always keeping it within earshot. I regularly check my compass. The ground cover underneath my feet is mostly wet leaves, several inches deep. I travel about a mile an hour, sometimes less. I travel as slow as I can – one carefully placed step at a time. More often than not, I hold onto the thin trunk of a young tree to keep my balance. I think about what would happen if I fractured a leg, about how long it would take someone to find me, and how much time would pass before anyone came looking for me in the first place. Not a pleasant thought. I move even slower, resisting the temptation to go charging downhill in leaps and bounds. Take it easy, I tell myself, take it easy... nice and slow. I stop to inspect a flower every now and then. I look around for some sign of human presence. Nothing. I look around for some sign of animal presence. No deer tracks, but there are some strange scars on the side of a tree. Bear claw marks maybe?

It occurs to me that, as the day gets brighter, my descent is even more rapid than I had expected it to be. The spruces and balsam firs have already yielded to hardwoods for the most part, and much light filters through tree branches to the forest floor. The slope is not so steep now, so I follow the brook closely as it turns to the east, linking up with feeder streams along the way. From a murmur, to a babble, to a roar! The brook gathers strength as it cascades over rocks endlessly downward, downward. In the middle of a copse of birches, I stop and listen. The rush of water through the woods makes a sound, which warms me inside, much the same way the voice of an old friend does when I hear it again after a long silence. I smile absently, then keep moving. Somewhere around two thousand feet, I come to a place where two major streams merge. I squat next to the brook and watch liquid as clear as glass pour over gravel-sized stones. I lean forward, splash the ice cold water on my face, then drink greedily with cupped hands. It drips from my beard as I sit back against a rock and nibble at my dwindling supply of gorp.

There's not much to the forest when you think about it. Earth, rocks, water, some vegetation, some wildlife – that's about it. And it's pretty much the same wherever you go. Variations on a theme, a few surprises here and there, but the same basic forest community, regardless. Some people say that if you've seen one patch of trilliums, you've seen them all. Now that may be true, but for some strange reason, I can't get enough of it. What is the real attraction here – peace and quiet? No, even the big city has places that provide that. What is it then?

Sitting at this fork in the brook, I enjoy the wonderful sensation of simply being – nothing special – just being in the woods… in the world. Time has stopped. I feel like an animal, clothed and carrying with me a bag full of food and various gadgets. Pretty basic, when you think about it. Nothing special at all. Just another animal footloose in the forest.

There are times when the mere sight of a wildflower opening in early spring can bring me to the verge of tears, but this is not one of them. Considering the natural beauty around me right now, I am extraordinarily indifferent to it all, happy to simply indulge myself in a luxurious idleness, completely carefree for the first time in a long, long while. I saunter over to a dead log to urinate. I poke at a strange-looking mushroom for a while, then return to the brook. What was my big reason for coming out here again? Whatever it was, it doesn't really matter anymore. Just being here is all that matters. Just being comfortable – in the truest sense of the word. Oh sure, I'm dirty and sweaty and achy and stiff in the lower back, shoulders and thighs, but I'm comfortable all the same. The forest is my living room without walls. Nothing bad can happen to me here. Nothing, that is, but what nature throws at me, and so far she has been quite friendly. Cool, dry air with overcast skies – a great day to be outdoors. No complaint.

Water drips from moss-covered rocks as it does from my beard. The heavy scent of decaying leaves hangs in the air like a dank perfume. The incessant crash of the brook washes away all concern. What else could I possibly want?

What's that? In the distance a sound – the low, woody notes of a flute. But no, it must be the wind whistling through a hollow log. But there's no wind. I listen more carefully for that sound again. Nothing. Perhaps it's only my imagination. Of course, of course. I'm getting a little spooked – it's time to get moving. "Can't stay here forever," I say out loud, and the sound of my own voice startles me.   Talking to myself already? Definitely time to get moving.   Another half a mile or so, find that road, make camp, then relax.   Will be able to daydream all I want once I find that road and make camp.

At first it is only the faint outline of what had been a logging road once, then it is a deer trail, then it is a bona fide footpath.   Suddenly the footpath turns into two parallel tracks cutting through a broad, flat corridor.   Although overgrown with grasses, shrubs and saplings, the tracks are easy to follow.   Any minute now I expect to stumble upon a road beaten down by four-wheel drive vehicles.   Already the woods reek of human presence: an absurdly large fire circle; a couple of discarded beer cans; a fallen tree hacked up by some yahoo pretending to be Daniel Boone; stones kicked over by clumsy feet; bright red hunter's ribbons tied to trees. . . No tire tracks or footprints, though. Evidently, the recent rains washed them all away.

Directly   ahead,   not   three   miles   away,   is Highway 100.   Civilization, what a concept.   I am ambivalent about it, to say the least. On one hand, I am relieved to have made it down the mountain without event – slipping on wet rocks a couple times, but with only a scratch on my forearm to show for it.   On the other hand, the possibility of an intrusion upon my solitude is no longer remote.   In fact, I may stumble across a group of campers any minute now.

A large mound of earth blocks the tracks just as they begin looking like they can support a pickup truck. On the other side of the mound is another one of those Breadloaf Wilderness signs, much like the one I saw yesterday, only this one has added to it: "No vehicles beyond this point." That makes me feel real good inside. It's nice to know that there are others who feel as I do about the forest. That such a sign exists is cause for celebration. Within sight of the sign is a vehicle turnaround – the end of the dirt road as indicated on my map. I backtrack a few hundred yards, find a flat spot near the brook. Someone has camped here before. The flat spot has a small fire circle in the middle of it.

After dropping my pack to the ground, I quickly survey the area to determine how water will run off the land when it rains again. The flat spot looks good, looks like just the place to be. I set up the tarp facing the brook, with one end close to the ground and the other end three feet high, making it look like a lean-to. I stretch out the groundcloth beneath it. Then I string a line between two trees and hang my wet clothes out to dry. Home sweet home.

7

After making camp, I gather twigs and fallen tree branches the width of my wrist, break them up, then pile them neatly underneath the tarp. A grey cloud looms directly overhead but drops no water, at least not yet. I've been fortunate so far today – a brief bout of rainlessness in an otherwise wet week. No problem starting a fire tonight, though, rain or no rain. The wood underneath the tarp will be dry enough to burn by sundown, and there is enough of it for two or three fires. Good. That means tea for certain tomorrow morning.

I eat cheese, pepperoni and crackers for lunch again, then check my fishing pole. Not good. At some point during this morning's descent, the tip of it broke off. Strange that I didn't notice. It must have snagged on a small tree or something as I was making my way through the dense underbrush. Using the black electrician's tape that I keep on hand for repairs, I attach the broken tip to the next section of my rod in a partially collapsed position. This shortens my rod by a foot. Can I still catch fish with this makeshift rig? Only one way to find out. After finishing lunch, I hike beyond the Breadloaf Wilderness sign, down the dirt road about a mile, then cut back over to the brook. I fish upstream from there, slowly working my way back toward my camp.

If fishing is a mania, then trout fishing is even more so. Because trout inhabit cold water, they have certain characteristics that set them apart from most other fish. They are lightning fast, strike the bait with more force than their size warrants, and put up one hell of a fight once they're hooked. Unlike most other fish, trout are quite adept at spitting out hooks. They work themselves free more often than not. Unlike most other fish, they are stunningly beautiful when first pulled from the water. Their colorful field markings and their sleek, torpedo-like bodies give them an otherworldly appearance.

It's great to be alive, to be creeping along the edge of a brook, rod in hand, hunched over, occasionally stopping behind rocks to look ahead. I slowly approach a pool of emerald green water fed by a small waterfall with grey boulders huddled around it. A cast five minutes earlier told the story – they are biting now and this pool will most likely produce a fair-sized brookie, maybe even a rainbow trout. If I present the bait properly, my first cast into this pool will lead to a powerful strike. The anticipation is exquisite. I painstakingly move into position – not too close – then raise my rod.

There's a long-standing rivalry among trout fishermen, between those who use live bait and those who use artificial flies. As a general rule, the fly fisherman is a sportsman interested primarily in the aesthetics of his avocation, while the bait fisherman catches fish in order to eat them. The fly fisherman stands thigh-deep in wide rivers meandering through meadows on sunny days. He cuts a fine picture for the covers of outdoor magazines. He catches big fish with coolness, great skill and finesse. By comparison (or so the fly fisherman will tell you) the bait fisherman is a hairy throwback running amok on the stream, a meat-eater who decimates the trout population. But at least the bait fisherman harbors no illusions about why he is there. True, there may be less sport in his method, but there is less pretense in it, as well. He is not out there to demonstrate the fine art of catching fish. Once the bait fisherman has hooked a trout, he lands it any way he can. After all, the trout is edible.

With enough worms in the bait box hanging from my belt, I hunt trout. High in the mountains, I stalk my prey, creeping upstream, stepping from one small rock in the brook to another, occasionally getting wet. Sometimes I use nightcrawlers that come in styrofoam containers, half-hidden in the beer coolers of country stores, but I prefer to use the worms and other terrestrials I find under rocks or in the banks of brooks.

A hook is not humane by any stretch of the imagination, but if it's small enough and a fisherman knows what he's doing, it does little damage to the fish. The trick is to hook the trout in the mouth only. Sometimes this is easier said than done. Sometimes the hook lodges deep into the gills of the fish and a bloody mess results. Sometimes fishing seems like the most barbaric of all sports.

Fishing is brutal, no doubt, but all the same it can make one feel grounded, connected to the earth. On this trip, I'm carrying a little less food than I need, expecting to get my dinner from the brook at least once. By placing myself in this situation, I enter into a relationship with nature that doesn't exist at the supermarket. Find the trout; keep from spooking him; present the bait; hook him; then land him. Hardly the same as pulling a can of tuna down from the shelf. And while all this is going on, the benign indifference of the forest permeates the air as the never-ending murmur of the stream fills my ears.

Out West, I used to go into the mountains with a half-breed Indian who insisted that we fish on empty stomachs. To have your mouth water when you get a hit undermines any noble idea about how you stand apart from nature. Sometimes my friend and I would feast; other times we would walk away from the brook hungry. Always both fish and fishermen had something at stake.

Ah, but today I am fishing with a full belly. My old Indian friend would be sadly disappointed in me if he knew. And yet the prospect of another pepperoni and cheese meal this evening is not the least bit appealing. I long for a trout dinner.

To my surprise, shortening the pole actually improves my fishing, enabling me to cast around the many obstacles cluttering the brook, into all the places where trout like to hide. The action of my rod is poor to be sure, but I catch fish with it anyway. I catch and release countless small brook trout; keep five mid-size ones for dinner.

I work my way upstream the better part of the afternoon, in no hurry, happy just to be there. A little moisture drops from the sky as I fish, but nothing substantial. Before long, I crouch in front of a familiar pool. Looking up, I see a tarp, a pack leaning against a tree and clothes hanging from a line. Back in camp already. A pleasant afternoon on the brook. After cleaning the fish, I tie them together by running a piece of string through their gills. Then I put them back in the water to keep them fresh until dinner, which, according to my stomach, is still several hours away.

Late afternoon, I poke around the woods, staying close to camp, studying flowers. Along the brook, I stumble upon some twinflower. There are purple and painted trilliums everywhere, of course. Within yards of the fire circle grows spring beauty; more wood anemone; wild strawberry; false Solomon's seal; blue, yellow and white violets; trout lilies; bellwort; and a host of other flowers I can't identify – my favorite being a small plant with tiny white flowers in tight clusters. Being unable to name it in no way diminishes its beauty, although I wish I had a better flower identification book. Evidently, there are far more flowers in New

England than the hundred or so portrayed in the thin volume I carry with me.

Could the Garden of Eden have been any better than this? Hard to believe. Sometimes I look around and imagine that we're still living in the Garden, that only our perception of it has changed. Perhaps paradise is but a state of mind. Wandering among the flowers, I am as close to paradise as I will ever be.

The incredible flexibility of nature boggles my mind, makes me seriously question our role in the greater scheme of things. Perhaps we are not as central as we like to think we are. Perhaps flowering plants play a more crucial role than we do. Whenever I wander through the forest, I can't help but wonder why we have such a distorted sense of self-importance. I inspect the flowers closely with a small magnifying glass. Their designs are so mysterious, so diverse – it suddenly occurs to me that anything is possible in this world. Absolutely anything. The startling complexity of the most common flower supports my suspicion that there are creative forces at work in the universe that dwarf our own meager efforts. The beauty of even a simple lily holds me transfixed – how fortunate to find myself in the presence of such a thing!

Evening early, back in camp. I start thinking about how good a cup of hot tea will taste. I improve my woodpile by breaking some of the larger sticks into shorter lengths, then separating them according to size. Too early in the day for a fire? As if time matters. As if I am on any kind of schedule. No hot food or liquid for two days – way overdue. And this dry wood promises to burn well.

8

Just as I am getting ready to start a fire, I look over and
see a man standing along the brook. He is wearing blue
jeans, a flannel shirt, work boots and a baseball cap. He
is fishing. I watch as he catches a small trout then
shakes it from his line. Disgust registers on his face. I
open my mouth to shout a "hello" at him but the word
doesn't come out. I move a little closer to the edge of
the bank, wait for him to notice me. A moment later he
looks up and to his surprise sees me standing there. I
wave at him with an open hand. He shouts a throaty
greeting which startles me. I respond weakly. He casts
his line a few more times, then crosses the brook and
walks over to me.

He is friendly enough, but his words seem
strained, his manner seems aggressive, and his voice
seems excessively loud and harsh. Although he stands
only ten feet away, the sound of his voice carries a
hundred yards through the woods, at least. What's his
problem?

The man is wound tightly. He has driven here
straight from work, no doubt. He is here for the
obvious reason: to relax, to take it easy. His forehead
is deeply furrowed with worry and his brows are
closely knitted together. Although he makes a
conscious effort to be friendly, his eyes betray both
sadness and anger bubbling just below the surface of
congeniality. I know the feeling all too well. In a
different time and place, I could be out for the evening
and he could be camped here along this brook. I feel
sorry for him; I feel a little guilty for having enjoyed a
day in the woods while he was trapped at some

workplace, deeply mired in the boredom of a daily routine.

Perhaps he is mad at me for spoiling the fishing on this brook. He noticed my fishing pole right away. I inform him that I've only fished as far up this brook as my camp, but noticed a few nice holes farther upstream when I hiked down the mountain this morning. He thanks me for the tip and then, after a moment of awkward silence, asks me if I've been following the Long Trail. I tell him that I hiked up the Cooley Glen Trail, then bushwhacked down the mountain to here. He nods his head but I can tell that he doesn't hike much, if at all. He cruised up the dirt road in a four-wheel-drive pickup truck and my guess is that he rarely gets too far away from either road or vehicle.

I wonder what he thinks of me. I must be quite the sight to behold. Real woodsy. My pants are filthy – the same ones I've worn since Thursday. My sweater has burs in it, which I see no reason to remove. A hunting knife dangles from my belt as naturally as a hammer from a carpenter's apron, but my manner isn't aggressive. In fact, if my camp weren't here, I would do what wild animals do: avoid him altogether. I think he senses this. My beard and hair are typically disheveled – he may think that I'm slightly insane, or a fugitive from civilization, or both. I don't look like your average camper, that's for sure.

Conversation is difficult when two people run into each other in the woods. The deeper they are in the forest when they meet, the harder it is for them to overcome that natural aloofness. Either both people make an extra effort to interact, or contact is quickly broken off. The fisherman and I choose the latter.

Neither one of us is here to socialize, so we cordially say our goodbyes. He returns to his fishing, slowly disappearing around the bend, as I go back to my fire-building. I hope for his sake that he catches a big enough fish to make his day, but it isn't likely. From what I observed, he's not interested in fishing, not really. Anyway, I build my fire, and neither see nor hear him later on when he returns to his truck.

Dusk already. With the fire burning nicely, I cook and eat the trout one at a time, then whip up some quick-and-easy Chinese noodles. A simple dinner. Afterward, I boil water for tea and it tastes wonderful. Just the thing needed. Later on, I rebuild the fire and boil more water to refill my water bottle. I drank directly from the brook all day, so it seems rather futile to purify water now, but I go through the motions anyway – more ritual than anything else.

The last vestige of light vanishes from the patch of sky overhead. The campfire becomes the center of my small universe. I stare into it as I stretch out on the ground with foam pad underneath me. I sip tea and chuckle to myself as I think about "roughing it" – as if camping out was nothing but hardship. What a good hobo I'd make! But what does a hobo do in the winter? Hmm...

Flames lick the pot; a green piece of wood sizzles. I poke at the fire with my trout-roasting switch. I add one of the larger sticks to it, another, and then another until I have a small bonfire going. Usually I won't build a fire any bigger than necessary, but after two days without one, it's time to indulge myself. There have been a few others camped here before me, but firewood is still readily available. At first I don't feel right about wasting fuel, but then it dawns on me that as long as I am willing to collect more wood in the morning, it doesn't matter. Besides, I need the dancing flames right now, need to gaze into the fire as a gypsy gazes into a crystal ball. My thoughts are flowing freely and I want to encourage them. I am curious to see what will emerge.

Funny what crops up. I start thinking about Judy, about how well we've been getting along these past few years, about how we ought to get married. I surprise myself with that. Suppose I am missing her, although I haven't noticed any particularly sharp pangs of loneliness. Absence, the heart, and all that. Wish she was with me now to share this campfire. She's a big one for staring into flames. Oh well. Will see her again in a couple more days. Will have to talk with her about marriage. See if she is still as interested in the prospect as she was a few months ago.

Other than that, no profound thoughts. I disappoint myself on that count. In fact, I am rather surprised at the sheer poverty of my musings, the absence of anything that can be considered even remotely philosophical. There is something about the wilderness that undermines the inclination towards speculative thought. Do we develop a natural complacency when we are in the woods? No, it's something else – a sense of immediacy that prevents abstraction. In the woods, the life of the mind is all too easily overwhelmed by the absolute present. But no matter. The way in which we live our lives is the important thing. The rest of it is only gibberish. And being alone in the woods, staring into the campfire is as meaningful a statement as any philosopher needs to make. It's an authentic statement, anyway. One can say or think anything, but ultimately it comes down to how one chooses to live.

It's difficult for me to believe that there is anyone in the world who couldn't enjoy a night like this, camped alone in the woods. Staring into the fire, I toy with the idea of putting together an organization that could provide people with the opportunity to try it. How absurd! As if those who really want to spend some time alone in the woods couldn't find a way to do so on their own. As if a wilderness experience could be packaged, then made available for a small fee. As if solitude had universal appeal, like gold or silver. No, it's not for everyone. Only a few people ever develop a taste for it. Best to simply count my blessings and leave it at that.

9

Morning early. Day four. After a leisurely breakfast, I go over to the edge of my camp to dig a small cat-hole, then empty my bowels. While squatting between two striped maples, I first notice it. Directly in front of me, not two feet away, standing tall yet inconspicuous because of its green, leaf-like body, is a fully matured Jack-in-the-pulpit. I lift the overhanging spathe to peer inside. Sure enough, there it is – that brown, phallic-looking spadix, poised like a minister on the verge of a sermon. Just beyond that Jack, I see another one, and then another. I pull up my pants, then go looking for more of those strange flowers. My camp is overrun with them. One grows not six inches from a stake holding down a corner of my tarp. I must have leaned over it while setting the stake in place. Incredible. We see only what we allow ourselves to see, or what we expect to see, or only that which is so obvious we can't avoid seeing it. Have I stepped on any without realizing it? Miraculously enough, all the Jacks in my camp are standing tall. God only knows how my boots missed them.

After this surprising discovery, I look around my camp with different eyes, discerning every detail like a hawk seeking its prey. I see nothing. Nothing, that is, but Jack-in-the-pulpits and a few other flowers. But isn't that enough surprise for one day?

Yet another humbling experience. Just when I think I'm Mr. Joe Wilderness, a flower puts me in my place. Not that I'm complaining. These Jacks are a nice addition to my camp, especially the one near the tarp, which stands tall like a sentry guarding over my belongings, like a silent yet faithful companion. While admiring its subtle beauty, I quickly forget my chagrin.

Rod in hand, I leave camp after cleaning up a bit. I walk halfway down the dirt road towards Highway 100, past the waterfall, past the bridge, beyond the closed-up cabin. Slipping through the brush, I come to a couple small cascading waterfalls and start fishing. With that fateful first cast, I begin a long series of rhythmic casting motions that flow from me as naturally as a yawn. The morning passes quickly.

Near the waterfall, I hook a rather large trout – one of the biggest in this brook, no doubt. He throws the hook as I try to reel him in, and then, as if dazed or disoriented, he hovers near center-bottom of a shallow pool not six feet away, in clear view. If I can see him, then he can see me, but when I cast my line into the pool, he rises to the bait anyway. I give the line a tug with a quick flick of the wrist in order to set the hook. No good. I throw the bait at him again; he rises to it again. Same story. We repeat this cycle three more times, at least. It is hard to say which one of us is being more thick-headed. Not once during this comedy are we out of sight of each other. I become as dazed as he is. And it takes every bit of self-control I can muster to refrain from diving into that pool after him with open, grasping hands. Mania. I want so badly to catch him, just to hold him in my hands... Why? God only knows.

I can't land the fish, but maybe it's for the best. We get to know each other during our prolonged struggle, him in his element, me in mine, with only that thin, filmy surface between us. Never before have I observed a trout so closely. I believe I could reach over and touch him. But I don't. Instead, I move on, hoping that he will live to a ripe old age. Making a meal out of him would have been a sad epilogue to such a contest. This way the myth lives on. The one that got away...

Lunch back at my camp – I wolf down whatever is handy. The black flies are swarming now. More cheese, pepperoni and crackers (ugh), then I grab my rod and I'm back on the move again. Insects constantly buzz around me, but somehow I notice them less when I have a rod in my hand. Amazing how the mind works. The air is dry and the flies are having a field day. I take many hits but try not to think about it.

After lunch, I have the dubious honor of witnessing a hatch of mosquitoes from a puddle of brackish water. They break the surface of the water then leap into the air. They aren't a problem yet, but soon will be. I keep moving.

I fish for several hours, although the thrill is gone. Going through the motions – more habit than pleasure. Cast, a bump, reel it in... cast, a bump, reel it in. I catch at least twenty fish. After a while, I stop counting. Put most of them back. "Educating fish" is what a friend of mine calls it – teaching the younger fish a lesson or two about how appearances cannot always be trusted. Good for the fish, perhaps, but I'm not getting any smarter.

Tired, just about ready to quit for the day but... just one more cast... and on and on like that for another half hour. There, a bump and then another bump, but me a little bit slow responding. With a clumsy jerk of the pole, I land a young trout no more than four inches long. I have hooked him badly. He bleeds at the gills. Unlike most other fish, a small brook trout is as good as dead once it's bleeding. They've no stamina in that respect – the delicacy of wild things. Although I have a pair of pliers in my back pocket, I realize that a careful extraction of the hook would be futile. What a waste. Too small to eat, as good as dead, and all because I haven't been paying attention. What a terrible waste! Frustrated, I tear the hook from the brook trout's mouth, then watch the fish die in my hand. I feel its spirit leave its body in one last, violent spasm. I toss the carcass back in the water to rid myself of it. Why does it always come down to this? Blood on the hands – a hell of a way to relate to nature. Some sport. I immediately collapse my pole and call it a day. Couldn't leave it alone. Had to push it to the limit. I tramp slowly back towards camp, brooding over the image burnt forever into my mind of a trout floating belly-up.

A little rain falls, but it doesn't last. The clouds break up, temps shoot well into the seventies, and both the black flies and the mosquitoes amass in overwhelming numbers. I drop off my fishing pole in camp and keep moving. This morning, I spotted what might be a hawk's nest – down the brook a quarter mile. I go back to check it out.

The nest is huge. It's big enough to accommodate me… if I could only get up the tree. No sound. No hawk. Abandoned maybe? Too big to be anything but a hawk's nest. Then again, it's hard to say. Perhaps some smaller bird is using it now. I keep moving.

I enter a stand of mature pines. It's cool and dark in here. Birds are in the tangle of tree limbs way above me. They are impossible to identify. I watch them for a while then move into a stand of hardwoods, looking for some new flower. Stumbling over a tree root, I just barely regain my footing before falling flat on my face. While catching myself, I smash the life out of a trillium with my big, dirty boot. A moment of desperation: I try propping up the flower by piling soil and dead leaves around it. No good. Broken. As good as dead. Tomorrow's humus. I slide into despair. A murderer on two counts now. What's the difference between me and a chemical manufacturer? Mine is a more hands-on approach. I go back to camp, to seek out Jack-in-the-pulpit, to confess my crimes to him and gain consolation.

Guilty as charged, Jack says, on both counts! I plead for a reduced sentence on the grounds that my intentions are sterling, that I simply hadn't known any better. It doesn't wash. Jack holds me fully accountable for my actions, and already the mosquitoes and black flies are doling out the punishment. I can, of course, escape justice by resorting to the little green bottle of bug dope which I keep on hand for such occasions, but Jack makes it clear to me that by using chemical protection, I would be showing my true colors. The choice is mine. Accept the punishment stoically or take the sleazy way out, complete with all the lame rationalizations so typical of my species. A hard choice. A moment of truth.

10

Towards the brook I run, cheating the hangman. With temps well into the seventies, a dip in the brook seems like the easiest way out of my predicament. Besides, I like the idea of being clean again. I go down to a nearby hole – the one from which I extracted a trout yesterday. After stripping down to bare skin, I toe-test the water. Amazing! Who could imagine that unfrozen water could be so cold? Actually, it isn't that bad. I stand ankle deep in it for two or three minutes before my feet go numb. The trick is mustering the courage to immerse my entire body in the liquid ice. From past dips in the mountain brooks, I know all too well what it will feel like. But still, the swarm of insects flying around me grows larger with each passing moment. I feel a definite sense of urgency with all my skin exposed to them.

I wade thigh-deep into the pool, stand there swatting away bugs a while, then finally take the plunge, allowing my knees to cave-in underneath me. Yowza! Ice cold! Quickly – a second plunge before I regain my senses! I splash around another half minute, hop out of the pool, then stand upon a rock, dripping wet, pink all over and giggling like a fool.

Wide awake now, I hoot like a drunken redneck and shake water from my hair like a dog. Vigorously, I towel myself dry. Looking around, I see those tiny blood-sucking monsters buzzing through the air in wide circles, but they don't land on me. I am safe for the time being. The surface temperature of my body is a good thirty degrees less than what it was five minutes ago. Enjoy it while it lasts. In another five minutes they'll be on me again, but I'll have a fire going by then.

A slight breeze blowing down the brook caresses my skin as I dress. I hold out a clenched fist, measure the distance between the sun and the distant ridgeline. One and a half fists. In an hour the sun will slip behind the mountain and the air will cool off rapidly.

I build a fire as I wait for a fisherman to wander up the brook. The fire crackles and water boils. Two pots of tea later – still no one. Temps drop considerably after the sun falls from the sky. In the short time it takes to fill my two water bottles, I put on an extra shirt and then a sweater. I walked around barefoot not too long ago, but am wearing my camp shoes and a thick pair of socks now. Mosquitoes are still a menace, but not nearly as bad as they were. I throw leaves on the fire to smoke them out of camp. With my clothes reeking of smoke, I cook and eat the only two trout I kept today. After dinner, I let the fire burn down to a few smoldering embers. Daylight lingers long after the air cools off, long after the mosquitoes quit biting. I sit against a tree, my thoughts adrift, listening to the constant flow of water in the brook nearby...

What's that – a flute? I listen carefully. Yes, no doubt, in the distance, what sounds like someone playing a flute. Pan is out there somewhere, not far beyond my camp. But no, it's just my imagination. Can't be a flute. The wind or a bird or something. Four days alone and already I'm a little woods crazy. Just my imagination, of course. Yet it sounds so real...

One night several years ago, while camped alone in the Cascades, I couldn't get to sleep because of wood elves. They were having a party somewhere upstream. I could hear them laughing, clinking beer mugs, and carrying on. They were just barely within earshot, so I couldn't make out what they were talking about. Maybe they were talking about me, who knows? Just my imagination, of course. Even then I knew it was only the sound of water breaking over rocks, but somehow that hardly mattered. Imagined or real, I still heard them. The forest casts it spell on you after you've been alone in it for a few days and haven't heard a human voice other than your own. It's interesting what a jumble the real and the imagined can become. You know the difference between the two, but it doesn't matter any more. You still hear the elves; you still hear the flute loud and clear.

Standing ankle deep in a pool of water years ago, I was mystified by the fact that it had no apparent outlet and yet a raging torrent cascaded into it from twenty feet above. There is a rational explanation, of course. Any scientist will tell you that the stream simply went underground at that point, and that the entrance to the cavern was so full of stones that I could stand on top of it. I suspected as much at the time, but that didn't diminish the sense of wonder I felt. God help me the day I'm no longer amazed by such things. What's the use in living once the world has lost all its mystery? Everything doesn't have to make sense – not all the time, anyhow. Who could bear it?

Darkness at last. I build up the fire, then lose myself in the flames. I feed it a few remaining sticks to keep it burning. It's a completely unnecessary fire. With water boiled, dinner cooked, bugs gone for the evening and enough candles to adequately light up my camp, it serves no purpose. But still, it provides a bit of comfort and gives me something to stare at. Well worth the trouble.

Time flies. As I add the last piece of wood to the fire, it occurs to me that I will be hiking out the next day. Strange how it goes. Seems like I just got here. Not quite ready to leave, but will I ever be ready? When I am hungry and completely out of food, maybe. Will be good to see Judy again, anyway. To kiss and hug her – can't think of anything that I want more right now. Five days alone in the woods is plenty. Three days is usually enough to cure what ails me. The rest is gravy. A hot shower – what a concept. Wonder how the store's doing? No, think about it tomorrow, not now. The real world can wait another day or two. It's not going anywhere.

That Jack-in-the-pulpit near the tarp, half-hidden in the shadows, looks bigger now than it did during the day. Stars appear beyond the treetops. They sparkle like glitter thrown to the heavens before being obscured again by clouds. A rustling in the leaves nearby – some small creature approaches camp. It smells the rancid cheese, most likely. Ah, must hang the food bag before going to bed. Will leave a few crumbs for visitors, but no more. Won't be able to sleep with a bunch of critters running around camp all night.

A cabin in the woods would be nice, real nice. If I had a permanent place along a brook like this, I could retreat to it whenever I needed to get back to the wild. Or is this an impossible dream? I must admit, something is lost once a camp is made permanent. The wild is no longer wild once a building has been erected in the middle of it. The wild becomes a bit more accessible, perhaps, but still, it's over there somewhere... not here. The very idea of wilderness presumes the absence of anything human. Ha! What a bind! Without realizing it, I corrupt what I want and need the most.

The campfire dies back to a pile of glowing embers. I'm tired, real tired. Too tired to think any more. Tomorrow is another day. Time for bed.

11

Monday morning early, I crawl out of bed, throw together a fire just big enough to boil a pot of water, then make some tea. Breakfast consists of what is left: an apple, a week-old bagel and some raisins. Still have a little pepperoni and cheese left over, as well, but I don't dare eat it. It wouldn't have gone bad if I hadn't eaten so much trout. No complaint on that count, though.

The sun burns brightly through the trees – the makings of a beautiful day in the woods. I have considered lingering, hanging around half the morning before moving on, but the black flies are already swarming. A quick spin around the woods, one last look at nearby flowers, then I pack up my gear. The time has come.

I start down the road at a steady clip – relaxed and fresh, humming rather loudly, occasionally breaking into song as I am likely to do when hiking alone through the woods. My pack is considerably lighter now with a four-day supply of food removed from it. I could easily hike ten miles today. Flowers along the road, sunshine in my face, what else could I ask for? A bit more time in the woods, perhaps.

The dirt road is less than three miles long. At the rate I am moving, I'll be out in an hour. A mile and a half down the road, I stop for an extended water break – not so much because I need it but because I see no reason to hurry. After all, I have all day to get back to town.

Sitting on a log, I finish off the last of my provisions: a handful of raisins. I watch a feeder stream cascade in a series of waterfalls down, down to the brook. To my right is that shallow pool where I encountered the-one-that-got-away yesterday. I go over to say goodbye. That old trout is well out of sight. Perhaps he watches me from underneath a rock. Certainly, he isn't sad to see me go.

The waterfall is particularly beautiful this morning. As I gaze at the cords of water twisting down to the brook, I promise myself that I will spend as much time as possible in the woods from now on. I think about how I brooded over the human condition a mere week ago. It seems rather foolish to me now. As long as there are pockets of wilderness into which we can escape every once in a while, all is not lost. As long as there are forested mountains and brooks full of trout and places where only a birdsong breaks the silence, then a solid basis for hope exists. It's foolish to try to solve all the world's problems, especially the philosophical ones. Do what we can and leave it at that.

The last leg of the trip. I hike the final mile and a half down the road as slowly as possible, resisting the steady pull of gravity. I stop several times to observe closely the flowers I haven't noticed before: foamflower, miterwort, and white baneberry to name only a few. Every day another flower blooms. Every day something to look forward to. What a great time of year!

Before long, I am hiking past a house being renovated, and then another house, and then another.

The dirt road comes to an end. Suddenly, I am standing on the shoulder of Highway 100. Cars whoosh past in a fury of wind and noise. Nearby, the Stetson Brook empties into the Mad River, which flows north through the valley along the road, in the direction I will hitchhike home. I remove the bandana from my head and the knife from my belt in an effort to look a little bit more civilized. I start walking. As cars pass, I turn around and stick out my thumb, but a half hour goes by before anyone stops to pick me up. So much the better. That makes the transition a little easier.

Two rides and two hours after stepping out of the woods, I stand in the middle of Burlington – lawnmowers roaring, jets passing overhead, traffic lights flashing and everywhere cars, cars, cars rushing to and fro. The madness of civilization, I mutter as I feel the first pangs of wilderness withdrawal. Am I ready for it?

The first fellow to give me a ride was a nervous Quebecois who talked almost as fast as he drove, telling me the story of his life in a broken English that I punctuated with an occasional nod. The second ride was a little less intense: a less-talkative computer consultant on his way to Burlington. With music blasting over the radio, we carried on the semblance of a conversation – me stumbling over my words and him sounding rather bored with life.

I feel extremely self-conscious as I walk that last half-mile to my apartment. In the woods, there's no clear-cut division between oneself and the world. In the city, there is no question whatsoever as to what is self and what is other. I walk down the sidewalk as if through an alien land. In every direction, there are carefully manicured lawns, box-like buildings and concrete pathways cut at right angles to each other. Definitely not my world, I tell myself... and yet it is.

Once inside my apartment, I experience the comfortable familiarity of home. I drop my pack and immediately begin emptying it. I toss everything into a big pile in the middle of the floor, much like the one I created six days ago – the difference being that this pile is wet, dirty, decorated with twigs and dead leaves. Suddenly my body aches all over. Fatigue sets in. Home now, I physically unravel in a way that would have been impractical during the past five days.

Judy pops in for lunch. She chats with me just long enough to make me glad I am back. Shortly after she leaves, I begin a spree of sensual indulgences, beginning with a hot shower. A glass of ice tea, some juice, a hot dog, potato chips, some more tea... "What a luxury," I think as I admire the stove. A flick of the switch and instant heat! Hot tea in three minutes! A long nap in a comfy bed, a little classical music on the radio... slowly, insidiously, civilization seduces me with all of its amenities. It's good to be home again.

The comics in the newspaper are entertaining; the weather reports over the past five days even more so. Not much humor on the front page, though. The world is pretty much the same mess it was a week ago. The details change but the story remains the same. Oh well.

The next day, I am back in the store again, crunching numbers, trouble-shooting the many small problems that arose during my absence, chatting with anyone who happens to stop by. Back in the routine, but I feel pretty good about it. My little woods vacation was just the thing needed. There remains only one last thing for me to do.

The pot I used to boil water still sits on the kitchen counter at home. The bottom of the pot is pitch black and reeks of the campfire. I intentionally didn't clean it right away. Staring out the window of my store, I wonder how much time will elapse before Judy will say something. Another day, or two... perhaps three. She's pretty good about that kind of thing. She knows how the smell of the pot triggers memories of the forest. Eventually though, it will get in the way – it will be just another thing which needs to be cleaned. Then I'll take a scrubby to it. Shortly thereafter, that restless feeling will build up inside me again, along with that vague despair which accompanies my preoccupation with the human condition. Shortly thereafter, I will have to get away again. I can never get enough of it, it seems. No matter what I do, there comes a time when only another trip by myself into the woods can save me from my own dark thoughts. Thank God for roadless areas, where a set of tracks across the forest floor is the only indication that a human being has been there.

SNOWSHOEING
IN THE HIGH PEAKS

What can a hiker do in late winter when there are several feet of snow on the ground? The answer to that question might seem obvious to anyone who has grown up in the North Country, but it took me a while to catch on. Just recently, I've learned that mid-March can be an excellent time of year to get outdoors even though everything is still covered with great piles of the white stuff. Just recently, I've discovered snowshoeing. Since I've never felt comfortable on skis, snowshoes have become a viable alternative to staying indoors and going stir crazy. You could say that I've taken up the sport out of sheer necessity.

Although I'm still a novice when it comes to snowshoeing, I joined my friend, Steve, and five other Vermonters at the Garden Parking Lot one Sunday morning for a three-day trek into the High Peaks. Planning the trip well in advance, Steve had reserved an ADK cabin halfway up the Johns Brook Valley for a couple nights. That made it possible for us to stay in the mountains without all the gear necessary for winter camping. When Steve asked me if I wanted to go, I said yes, absolutely. I jumped at the chance to enjoy nature in winter for more than just a few hours at a time.

After strapping the last few pieces of stray gear onto our packs with bungee cords, we started up the trail in twos and threes. Those with cross-country skis quickly forged ahead while the rest of us brought up the rear, plodding along steadily on snowshoes. The sky was solidly overcast but no wind stirred. The air temperature held in the mid-twenties. It was a perfect day to be in the woods. Since no major changes in weather had been predicted for the next few days, we looked forward to mounting the Great Range during our trip.

Our two-hour jaunt to the cabin was relatively easy despite packs heavily laden with food and supplies. The snow underfoot was a solid, hard-packed surface all the way. Cross-country skiing remains a popular winter sport in the North Country and there's been a sudden surge of interest in snowshoeing lately. As a result, the trail we followed had been packed by scores of backcountry travelers who had gone before us.

We must have passed a dozen groups on their way out – far more people than we'd see during the rest of our outing. Timing is everything. Since we were starting our trip when most people were finishing theirs, we would have the Adirondacks largely to ourselves over the next couple days. A mass exodus was well underway by the time Steve, Jim and I had gone a mile from the parking lot. By the time we reached the cabin, most of the weekenders had cleared out of the area altogether.

Lunch was almost over when I straggled into the cabin a half hour behind the seasoned skiers in our group. An unfolded topo map covered the table and everyone was talking about a quick dash up the Great Range that afternoon. Which summit? Which route? Being a dozen pounds overweight and new to winter travel, I was a bit daunted by the prospect of climbing any mountain that afternoon. I thought we were going to rest up for a big climb the following day, but my companions convinced me that fair weather is a rare event in the mountains this time of year. Go when you can. I wolfed down a sandwich and followed everyone else out the door. A consensus had been reached. Saddleback was the most accessible peak.

Some people survive the cold season simply by hunkering down, keeping close to the hearth. They wait patiently for spring. Growing up in Ohio, that's what I used to do, anyhow. But winter is long in the North Country, so I changed my survival strategy a few years after moving here. I quickly learned to get outdoors whenever the opportunity arose. I went hiking whenever I thought the snow was crusted over enough to support my weight. Unfortunately, I was usually wrong about the condition of the snow's surface. More often than not, I would slog my way to exhaustion, post-holing through several feet of the white stuff for a mile or so before calling it quits. Since wading through snow isn't exactly my idea of fun, I investigated other modes of winter travel. Eventually, I came around to the only practical alternative to those long, thin, slippery boards called skis: I rented some snowshoes.

My first experience on snowshoes was pleasant enough, but cutting a new trail through fresh snow turned out to be a lot more work than I thought it would be. My second outing, along a well-groomed trail after a gentle overnight snowfall, occurred on a sunny day when the air was so still that I could hear a bird singing a mile away. I floated through deep green hemlocks casting blue shadows across pure white powder. I marveled at tree trunks etched sharply against the sky – vivid brown and dark gray lines in dazzling light. Epiphany! In an instant I converted to the cult of snowshoeing. Before the last of the snow melted that season, I had my own pair.

There are several different kinds of snowshoes on the market these days. The most popular variety is a short, narrow, plastic-and-aluminum snowshoe with steel claws underneath to grip icy surfaces or hard-packed snow. This somewhat expensive, high-tech snowshoe can be found in most mountain shops. They're all the rage. While they aren't particularly effective in deep powder, they work quite well on the hard-packed trails that most winter travelers tend to use. On the other hand, old timers still cling to the traditional snowshoe – the kind made with wood and rawhide. This variety usually shows up at flea markets and yard sales during the summer. Because they're much longer and wider than the newer snowshoes, they work better on flat or rolling terrain covered with deep powder. Unfortunately, they're not particularly effective on steep, icy slopes.

My snowshoes are called Green Mountain Bear Paws. They are manufactured by an outfit in Stowe, Vermont. Being a hybrid snowshoe, they're long enough to support my weight in deep powder, yet narrow enough for the trails. Since they're made with traditional materials, rawhide and wood, they suit my old fashioned tastes as well. It's a good all-purpose snowshoe – ideal for guys like me who want to go everywhere.

Monday morning, day two. We were on the move again. One member of our group stayed behind at the cabin – his knees having taken all the punishment they could handle while coming down Saddleback. The rest of us headed for the summit of Mt. Haystack – six miles away and three thousand feet above the cabin. The Rose brothers, along with a couple others in our group, had attempted Haystack the previous winter but had been forced back by sub-zero temperatures and high winds. This time there were no such obstacles. The temperature remained in the high twenties. No wind blew. A couple inches of fresh snow had accumulated overnight but no one seemed too concerned about it. We were confident about reaching the summit that day. The group was confident, that is. Personally, I wasn't quite sure if I was equal to the task. The first day's effort had taken a great deal out of me.

We moved up the trail mostly without words, reserving our energy for the task at hand. Deep snow transformed the low roar of the brook to a murmur. Bird songs were few and far between. The skrunch, skrunch of our snowshoes seemed unnaturally loud. The clean intensity of the cold air reaching deep into my lungs made me feel more alert than I thought possible in the end of winter. Month number five of the cold season and still it maintained some of its original allure. I was amazed by it. A few more outings like this and my generally negative attitude towards winter might fade away completely.

Snowshoes were as much a part of the aboriginal way of life in these Northeastern woodlands as the birch bark canoe. The first people migrating to North America from Siberia thousands of years ago brought snowshoes with them. The first Europeans to use snowshoes were probably Vikings scratching out a living for themselves along the frozen Labrador coast. In the 17th Century, French Canadian voyageurs traversing the subarctic and Englishmen trading around the Hudson Bay no doubt learned about snowshoes from Cree and Algonquin peoples. The Abenaki and the Iroquois probably introduced snowshoes to the English settlers of New England and New York. Roger's Rangers – that renowned band of New Hampshire militiamen – employed snowshoes during the French and Indian War. In March of 1758, they fought the French and their Algonquin allies in the Lake George region of the Adirondacks atop four feet of snow in what's now known as the Battle of Snowshoes.

As the bird flies, Lake George is only forty miles southeast of the Johns Brook Valley. As the six of us slowly, arduously worked our way up the Great Range, the French and Indian War seemed light years away. Yet we propelled ourselves over the snow the same way Native Americans and frontiersmen had done for centuries.

Haystack isn't easily accessible. From any direction, it's a long hike to the top. At 3,500 feet, I started losing steam. Just above 4,000 feet, I felt a spasm in my left thigh. After negotiating a rather steep pitch just below Little Haystack, my leg began to cramp. That was the end of the climb for me. The rest of the group seemed no less exhausted, but somehow they were all able to keep going. I assured Steve that I'd be all right, ambling slowly back down the trail by myself towards the cabin. He assured me that he and the others would be on my heels shortly. With that justification, I did what I had been wanting to do since our departure from the parking lot the day before: I cut away from the group for an hour or so of luxurious backcountry solitude.

A great deal of snow had fallen during the previous two months. Not quite record-breaking amounts but getting there. On our way up the Great Range, trail markers nailed to trees six feet above the ground had sunken into the snow. I rediscovered them on my way down, along with the semblance of a hard-packed trail. All around me the green boughs of conifers drooped with the weight of wet snow. Stopping to catch my breath, I noticed the absolute silence of the forest. Only the occasional snap of a dry twig or the muffled thump of snow landing upon snow compromised it.

The tracks of snowshoe hares crisscrossed the trail for miles, convincing me that they were enjoying a banner year. Evidently, their predators can't get around nearly as well in such deep powder. A woodpecker knocked on a dead tree; the swollen buds of hobblebush and moosewood protruded through the snow. Spring wasn't far away. The tiny cones of great hemlocks have been strewn across the snow's surface like woody dice. The lonely call of a chickadee, a song quite common in these mountains even in deep winter, suddenly sounded to me like the harbinger of a new season. The gurgle of hidden rivulets carrying snowmelt down the Johns Brook seemed like another sure sign of imminent transition. I sweated even as I eased gradually downhill. The day grew warmer with air temperatures threatening to break the freezing mark. Suddenly it dawned on me that this would probably be my last snowshoeing trip the season. The snow would soon melt away. For the first time ever, I felt a tinge of sadness at the prospect of spring. Getting outdoors regularly on snowshoes was changing my perspective on things.

That evening in camp, the faces gathered around the dinner table were all glazed over with fatigue. To my mild surprise, I suddenly realized that I had more energy left than anyone else. So I grabbed the buckets to fetch water for cooking and cleaning. The cut in the snow down by the brook was at least four feet deep. I approached it warily. The Johns Brook flowed steadily beneath the snow. I couldn't help but wonder how Native Americans survived winter as well as they did when even fetching water required a good deal of effort and caution. Perhaps one simply grows accustomed to such minor, daily ordeals.

Later on that night, I slipped outside once again to look for stars among the trees and catch an earful of that incredible deep-woods silence. In the summer, the Adirondacks seem almost tame. But on dark winter nights like this one, when a Great Unknown prevails in the forest, these mountains seem utterly wild. Although the air was still, I could hear the wind howling through high mountain passes many miles away. When the distant wind subsided, I held my breath to keep from being distracted by the sound of my own breathing as I listened even more intently. Cold, dark stillness... It was quiet enough for me to hear the trees creaking even though they were hardly moving.

On our way out the next day, we passed half a dozen young men on their way to Slant Rock Shelter. They marched up the mountain in blatant disregard for the contrariness of winter weather. They had neither skis nor snowshoes. Granted, the trail was packed well enough to walk upon, but a quick thaw could quickly turn the hard snow beneath their feet to slush. A whiteout could make even a well-marked trail difficult to follow in broad daylight.

It's amazing how quickly I've come to rely upon my snowshoes. Now I can't imagine being without them. And while I still prefer the roughest hike through hot, heavily vegetated woodlands to an easy trek across open snowfields, I'm quick to take advantage of any opportunity I get to strap on my 'shoes. Without a doubt, snowshoeing requires a great deal more effort than hiking or skiing, but it's a mode of winter travel that suits guys like me quite well. A slow, steady, resolute moving forward... Snowshoes make it possible to go just about anywhere during winter – the more snow the better.

FOLLOWING THOREAU
TO KATAHDIN

1

Katahdin towers over the narrow tree-lined highway, dominating the surrounding landscape, giving one the impression that it is the only mountain of consequence in northern Maine. Its huge wall of grey rock renders me and my companion mute after the 400-mile drive from our native Vermont. We have arrived. We have just passed through Millinocket, the last town on this road, and are headed north by northwest into one of the largest pockets of wild country east of the Mississippi. A second paved road, built by the Great Northern Paper Company to accommodate its overloaded logging trucks, runs parallel to the one we're on. Aside from that, there is nothing but the occasional dirt road lined with recreational camps to disrupt the vast expanse of mountains, lakes, streams and woods from here to Baxter State Park and beyond.

A year and a half ago, I approached my friend and fellow outdoor adventurer, Charlie, with a proposal.

Would he be interested in retracing Thoreau's first excursion into the Maine Woods, paddling up the West Branch of the Penobscot River, then climbing Mt. Katahdin? He certainly was, but there was no craft available for such an outing. The Klepper, Charlie's two-man folding kayak, was languishing in the basement after years of disuse. Charlie also owns a multi-hulled fiberglass boat, but the rocky river bottom would give it a terrible beating. The two of us had shared some good times in the old Klepper. I thought a Maine paddle might be the just thing to do before easing the old workhorse into retirement. Its rotting canvas deck would have to be replaced first, though. I told Charlie that I'd help pay for the renovation. He quickly warmed to that idea, so we made plans.

Being masters of procrastination, we waited another year and three months before shipping the canvas and rubber shell of the Klepper to Colorado for repair. The job took longer than expected. July slipped away, then August. As our September 21st departure date drew closer, we began to worry. Labor Day came and went, still no Klepper. Charlie made some phone calls. We proceeded with logistical plans, but without a boat it all seemed rather moot. My wife bet me a six-pack of beer that the trip would have to be postponed. She lost the bet. The boat arrived via UPS, two days prior to departure. That gave us only one day to check it over, make sure we had all the parts and practice assembling it. One day was enough, though. Early this morning, Charlie and I folded up the Klepper and stashed it in a rental car along with all our gear and a week's worth of supplies. Then we left for Maine.

Our knowledge of central Maine is spotty. We have plenty of maps and guidebooks but lack the kind of practical knowledge that comes only from firsthand experience. A week ago, I learned from a phone conversation with a Maine resident that most of the West Branch of the Penobscot River above Ambajejus Lake runs too swift to paddle against. Thoreau and his party had poled their bateau up that portion of the river. Retracing their route in our kayak might be a bit more difficult than originally thought. We are willing to give it a try but have devised several alternate plans just in case. We are here to enjoy a week's worth of paddling and hiking – that's the main thing. It doesn't really matter where we go or what we do. Still, I'd like to see as much of Thoreau's route as possible, having read his account of it in *The Maine Woods* several times.

Early Sunday evening, Charlie and I reach a boat launch on the narrow strip of land between Millinocket Lake and Ambajejus Lake, about eight miles north of Millinocket. We had planned to insert our boat above the dam just west of town, but found the access road roped off and nowhere to leave our rental car. Here at the narrow strip, there is ample parking next to a general store, across the street from the boat launch. It will be an excellent place to leave the car and enter the watery realm tomorrow.

Late evening, too tired to find better place, we guerilla camp in an abandoned sandpit near the end of a dirt road. From the sandpit, it's a short walk to Deep Cove where we gaze upon Katahdin – a shadowy giant looming over the water. A waxing moon rises behind us, illuminating the rippled lake between the rocky shoreline and the mountain. We share a bottle of red wine in the water-lapping quiet. The temperature drops quickly through the 60s and 50s under a clearing sky. The mountain beckons us, but Charlie and I agree that a short paddle across Ambajejus Lake is the thing to do first. The mountain can wait.

On August 31, 1846, Henry David Thoreau took a break from his two-year experiment in simple living at Walden Pond and went north to sample nature at its wildest. His cousin, George Thatcher, was a Bangor lumberman headed upstream to look at some land. Aware of Henry's keen interest in nature, Thatcher asked him to come along. Thoreau started the journey alone, traveling by rail and steamboat to Bangor, Maine. On the first day of September, he and his cousin went by horse and buggy from there to Mattawankeag Point. They picked up two of Thatcher's friends at Mattawankeag. With a traced version of Greenleaf's rather sketchy map of Northern Maine, the foursome set forth on foot. They followed the Penobscot River another eighteen miles, tramping through the woods to "Uncle George" Macauslin's place where they hoped to hire Indian guides to take them farther.

The Indians never showed. After a day at Macauslin's place, waiting out some bad weather, they persuaded Uncle George to be their guide. He had been a river driver on the West Branch of the Penobscot for half a dozen years but was now content to provide supplies for the logging operation farther upstream. From his place it was another four miles to Thomas Fowler's house at the mouth of the Millinocket River on the West Branch, near modern-day Millinocket.

There they picked up an old bateau. Since the bateau required two experienced boatmen, Fowler was also talked into going, thus completing the party of six.

They exchanged their old, leaky bateau for a new one at "Old Fowlers" place, after a two-mile detour up the Millinocket River. Then they portaged to a spot just above the Grand Falls where the trip began in earnest. Tom Fowler and Uncle George poled the bateau up a small set of rapids, then everyone took turns paddling across the relatively calm waters of Quakish Lake. The two boatmen poled up another mile of rapids to a dam. A cook inhabiting the muddy logging camp near the dam served hot tea to the travelers. At that point, they were roughly a hundred miles upstream from Bangor. Even though it had already been a long journey, their excursion into the uninhabited part of the Maine woods was just beginning. After tea, they entered the Pemadumcook chain of lakes, going another five miles by moonlight to the head of North Twin Lake before stopping to make camp. Of this campsite, Thoreau wrote: "No face welcomed us but the fine fantastic sprays of free and happy evergreen trees, waving one above another in their ancient home." It was, for all practical purposes, Thoreau's first night in a bona fide wilderness.

2

Monday, mid-morning. Charlie and I have just unloaded the car and are busy reassembling the Klepper in a small grassy area next to the boat launch. It takes about an hour to hook together the numerous parts of the Klepper's wooden frame, slip the heavy rubber and canvas skin over it, then tighten it all up. A few fasteners are missing here and there so we do a bit of lashing to hold the boat together. Then we blow air into the spontoons – elongated flotation tubes located just beneath the canvas decking – to guarantee the boat's buoyancy. The brand new royal blue canvas decking looks sharp. It is so tight that a stone bounces off it like a quarter off an army recruit's bed. We are pleased. After easing the boat into the water, we pack all of our gear into it as rehearsed a couple days earlier and away we go, paddling nonchalantly across the dark amber waters of Ambajejus Lake.

The Klepper was invented by a German craftsman, Johannes Klepper, back in the 1930s. Johannes designed the lightweight, foldable boat so that it could be broken down and carried in two bags on the train that he took into the mountains. Upon reaching his destination, he would reassemble it and paddle back down to the lowlands.

The Klepper is a seaworthy craft, surprisingly stable, capable of taking on three-foot waves, as Charlie and I had the pleasure of learning back in the 80s. Charlie has paddled the Klepper in the Caribbean, along the Maine Coast and across the temperamental waters of Lake Champlain. It is patterned, of course, after the skin-covered sea kayaks that Inuits used in the arctic for centuries.

With its wooden frame and canvas decking, the Klepper retains much of the original kayak's character. The newer, much sleeker fiberglass kayaks are all the rage these days, but they lack the charm of this old boat. The Klepper's joints creak as it rides the swells, making it seem more like a creature of the deep than of human artifice. At first the creaking is a bit unsettling, but you come to love that sound once you're convinced that the boat isn't going to fall apart. The craft is more fluid than rigid, like the water itself. Being in it is an elemental experience.

Charlie controls the boat from the stern; I provide power from the bow. We use our binoculars and topographical maps to get our bearings during a short break on an island only a mile from the boat launch. Then we paddle northwest towards the wooded horizon where the West Branch of the Penobscot River enters Ambajejus Lake. It's a cool, mostly cloudy September day and the lake is all ours. A brisk wind creates a slight chop on the water's surface. Charlie and I get a little wet from spray but that doesn't matter since we're covered head-to-toe in raingear. A crimson blush here and there in the otherwise pale green forest lining the lake gives the day a distinctly autumnal feeling. The warm season is fading but it's still great to be out here. Our nerves unravel with each rhythmic stroke of the cupped paddles. We leave a slight wake in the water behind us as we reach what Charlie calls "escape velocity."

Mount Katahdin fills the northern horizon. The string of camps lining the shore, trailing away from the boat launch area, fades to infinite green. Directly ahead, a whitewashed building emerges from the forest. It looks like a remote frontier outpost, complete with an American flag flying high on the pole in front of it. The elderly gentleman who came down to chat with us earlier, while we were preparing to launch, mentioned an old logging-camp-turned-museum on an island near the mouth of the river. That must be what we see before us. We paddle up to a landing, then go ashore to check it out.

The sign affixed to the building reads: Ambajejus Boom House (1835-1907). Oddly enough, there is no mention of it in Thoreau's account. We call out but no one answers. The door is open so we step inside. In the process, we step back a hundred and fifty years to a time when only Penobscot Indians and a handful of loggers roamed the Maine Woods. I half expect some gruff old river driver to suddenly appear, asking us what we're doing here. Although clearly a museum now, with assorted logging tools displayed in nice tidy rows, the place still has that lived-in feeling. It is easy to imagine the crew out working somewhere, and a cook puttering about the busy-looking kitchen. They might appear any minute now. Upstairs there are clothes neatly unfolded on the bunks and playing cards on the table. The walls are covered with pictures of a bygone era – hearty men muscling huge logs downstream to great booms, where they are collected before being drifted to the sawmills.

A skiff motors to the landing, confirming our suspicion that someone was just here a few minutes ago. Instead of a burly river driver, the museum's caretaker steps out of the boat with an armload of supplies. After introducing himself and stashing his supplies, he explains how Thoreau and his party had paddled around a small island in the stream because that was the only way to get up the river back then. Ripogenus Dam, some twenty-odd miles upstream, has changed the character of the river since Thoreau's time. The West Branch runs higher, deeper and faster then it used to. Charlie and I are a little surprised by this news. Eager to explore as much of the river as we can, we return to the Klepper and resume our journey. We paddle upstream, against the steady current, about a half mile before encountering a small rapid just below Ambajejus Falls. It stops us cold. We fight the current for a while, nosing the Klepper into the riffles like a spawning salmon, but it's a lost cause. I had hoped to get a few miles upstream – perhaps within striking distance of Mount Katahdin – but Charlie makes it clear that we'd be towing the boat or portaging most of the way. So we turn the Klepper around and float effortlessly downstream, falling back on an alternate plan to circumnavigate Ambajejus Lake.

Following the uninhabited, western shore of Ambajejus now, we get a better sense of what this country must have been like a century and a half ago. Except for the coming and going of an amphibious plane, we are on our own. There are no boats anywhere in sight. Just the two of us, a rock strewn shore and the occasional passing loon. A great silence envelops us. I have been in wilder places, but few so disarmingly quiet. A strong breeze slips across the lake and into the conifers. In the Maine Woods, wild nature is alive and well.

We paddle southward towards open water, coming to a spit of land separating Ambajejus from the much larger Pemadumcook Lake. Here we stretch our legs before resuming the paddle. Then we turn east, dashing across one and a half miles of rolling water, the broadest part of Ambajejus, to the island where we stopped before. And the circuit is complete. With the Klepper beached, we unload and set up camp.

The island is about a hundred feet wide and perhaps three times that long. There are a few poplars and firs amid the rocks and a nice, sandy beach on the leeward side facing the bay. It's only a half-mile dash to the boat launch if we awaken to whitecaps tomorrow. Good thing. A landlubber at heart, I'm uncomfortable being surrounded by water.

Dusk comes all too quickly. Dinner is an expedient affair on the beach. A loon laughs in the distance; a wood duck floats through the darkness, begging for food. Charlie collected some birch bark earlier in the day, so we enjoy the semblance of a fire while basking in a sense of freedom that only wild country provides. Charlie rations the bark to the small bright flame to make it last as long as possible. As the last glimmer of light fades, a pale moon rises on the southern horizon. Water laps calmly to the sandy shore. To the north, Mt. Katahdin slowly disappears beneath a blanket of billowy, white clouds.

On the second day out of Old Fowler's place, Thoreau's party made good progress paddling their bateau up North Twin Lake, across the Deep Cove of Pemadumcook and into Ambajejus Lake. Thoreau was impressed with Ambajejus, commenting in his narrative that it was the most beautiful lake he had seen so far. No doubt Mt. Katahdin, clearly visible on the northern horizon, had something to do with that assessment. But he was even more impressed with the navigational skills of Uncle George – the only one in their party other than Fowler who had been this deep into the wild.

In his book, *The Maine Woods*, Thoreau wrote: "We could not but confess the importance of a pilot on these waters. While it is a river, you will not easily forget which way is up stream; but when you enter a lake, the river is completely lost, and you scan the distant shores in vain to find where it comes in."

Uncle George found the mouth of the West Branch and, with the help of the equally skilled boatsman, Tom Fowler, negotiated another nine miles of rough river before calling it a day. "We rowed across several small lakes, poled up numerous rapids and thoroughfares, and carried over four portages," Thoreau reported. A Herculean task by any measure, their excursion was even more remarkable when you consider how untrammeled the country was back then. The portage trails couldn't have been more than narrow, rocky paths winding through the dense brush.

Shortly after bypassing Abol Falls, they reached the mouth of Abol Stream. There they made camp and caught trout for dinner. Mt. Katahdin peeked above the trees, only half a dozen miles away as the bird flies. What a shock it must have been for our backyard naturalist. Almost a week out of his native Concord and over a hundred miles from the edge of civilization, it must have seemed to him like they had reached the end of the earth.

3

Tuesday morning, Charlie and I break camp in a hurry. We have a mountain to climb. I was told a few months ago, though, by those who had unsuccessfully attempted Mt. Katahdin, that a hiker has only a one-in-three chance of reaching its summit this time of year. Due to the mountain's notoriously foul weather, the rangers inside Baxter State Park frequently cut off access to the mountain. A ring of clouds obscures the top third of the mountain from view. The light rain that fell here last night could have been much heavier on the summit.

A short paddle gets us back to the boat launch by mid-morning. Spying a small, out-of-the-way beach next to the Katahdin Air Service building, we ask the owner if we can leave our Klepper there for a couple days. No problem, he says, so we transfer our gear from the boat to the car, saying goodbye to the water for a while.

At the park entrance, a ranger informs us that we can't hike up Mt. Katahdin today. Since there's a daily camping fee as well as a park entrance fee, Charlie and I decide against entering the park. We'll camp outside the park, waiting until we have a good shot at hiking the mountain. We noticed on our way to the park an abandoned-looking road that, according to our map, goes straight to a privately owned campground near the mouth of Abol Stream. We head that direction.

The barely paved road, pocked with potholes, was once a major thoroughfare for overloaded logging trucks. Now it's almost impassable. We park our car at a locked red gate, next to a trail marker for the Appalachian Trail. On the other side of the gate is a brand new logging road coming in from another direction. We load up our daypacks and follow it westward.

The new road passes the private campground then crosses the West Branch of the Penobscot. From the bridge we can see a fly fisherman on a sandy beach at the mouth of Abol Stream – the site where Thoreau and his party must have camped and fished a hundred and fifty years before. The relative tameness of this place comes as something of a shock to me, but it is no less beautiful than imagined. A cormorant rests on a rock protruding from the river. The morning sun casts our shadows over the clear water of the West Branch, urging me to go back to the car to get my fishing rod. But no, Charlie and I are in hiking mode now, so we finish crossing the bridge, turn down a dirt road on the opposite side of the river and follow it downstream to Abol Falls.

One look at Abol Falls and we're convinced that we made the right decision yesterday when we abandoned our upstream paddle. Poling a bateau is one thing; paddling a kayak is another. The river's current below the falls runs strong, very strong. Hiking farther downstream to Pockwockamus Falls, we marvel at the sheer force of water gushing through a narrow flume. It's a wonderful thing to behold, certainly, but we wouldn't want to be shooting that torrent. Thrashing through the dense brush around the falls with a kayak and gear is an even less appealing prospect. I think of Thoreau's party, that unwieldy bateau of theirs and the effort that they must have made to negotiate this obstacle. By comparison, Charlie and I seem to lack resolve.

A couple hours later, after a short detour to the nearby Hale Pond, we settle into a campsite near Abol Falls. Dinner is a brief affair. We build a small fire to warm ourselves afterward, finishing what's left of our bottle of red wine while pondering the various approaches to Katahdin's summit, Baxter Peak. Then we walk down to the river to catch the gleam of moonlight on water before calling it a day.

A blue jay serenades us at dawn. The patter of tiny raindrops against my tarp and distinct chill in the air makes it hard to get out of bed. Charlie isn't moving very fast either. It takes the better part of the morning to break camp, hike to the car and drive back to the park entrance.

At the park entrance, we are told that the treacherous Knife Edge Trail has been closed, but the rest of the trails up Katahdin are open if we want to hike into the clouds today. We decide against it, hoping that the sky will clear tomorrow as promised by weather forecasters. In the meantime, we'll entertain ourselves with a drive along the perimeter road that snakes northward, deeper into the forest, skirting the westernmost edge of Baxter State Park.

In 1917, a wealthy lumber baron named Percival Proctor Baxter tried to talk the Maine legislature into buying land from the logging companies in order to preserve Mt. Katahdin and the mountainous country just north of it. Even though his initial, one-man campaign wasn't successful, he continued to lobby for the protection of the area when he became the governor of Maine in the 1920s. Still no success. After his short stint as governor, he took matters into his own hands, buying up the land around the mountain and organizing it into a park. He established a trust fund so that the park would always be self-sustaining. Eventually, he donated the land to the people of Maine and thus Baxter State Park came into being – 200,000 acres of wild country right in the heart of the Maine Woods. Because of its quasi-independent status, Baxter State Park is managed somewhat differently from other public lands. Park rangers exert greater control over it for one thing. They open and close the trails on Katahdin at will, in accordance with the whims of nature. While this frustrates many would-be climbers, it radically reduces the number of mountaineering accidents. Due to its size and close proximity to the ocean, Mt. Katahdin has a unique and rather volatile microclimate, making it second only to Mount Washington as the most dangerous mountain in the Northeast. Yet hikers do not perish as frequently on the former as they do on the latter. No doubt other state and national parks will follow the Baxter State Park management model in the future. This is a good thing, I suppose, but I can't help but feel that an integral part of the wilderness experience has been lost in the process.

4

In 1804, a surveyor named Charles Turner Jr. and his party climbed Mt. Katahdin. They were the first white men to do so. In 1816, a slide at the head of Abol Stream tore away a strip of soil and vegetation, creating an easy route up the mountain. The slide, located on Katahdin's southwestern slope, is clearly visible from the West Branch of the Penobscot. That made it the obvious choice for Thoreau and his companions, who were among the first few climbing parties to ever attempt the mountain.

Since no one in Thoreau's party had climbed the mountain before, they had no idea just how far they'd have to hike from the river in order to reach the summit. Uncle George made a guess, based upon what he'd heard from other river drivers: about four miles. After the hike, Thoreau figured it "nearer fourteen." Using the detailed topographical maps available today, I reckon the distance to be somewhere between eight and ten miles. No small task, considering that the trail they took wasn't much of a trail at all – a bushwhack for the most part, following the tracks of animals.

On September 7th, Thoreau's party stashed their bateau and set forth on foot. "By six o'clock, having mounted our packs and a good blanketful of trout," Thoreau wrote, "We started for the summit of the mountain." They followed Abol Stream as far as they could. Soon they were encountering the telltale signs of bear and moose – scat, rubbings, tracks, etc – but none came into view. Eventually they crossed Murch Brook, better known today as Katahdin Stream. Then they stopped, making camp along a feeder stream late in the afternoon, fearing that they would run out of water if they went any farther. While the rest of the party made camp, Henry scouted ahead, hoping to catch a glimpse of the summit. He didn't get very far before turning back.

The next day, Thoreau's party made a play for the summit, ascending via Abol Slide. Thoreau took the lead, charging ahead until he lost sight of his companions. Although it was a clear day everywhere else, the summit was shrouded in clouds. Thoreau entered the fog alone, scrambling over the rocks until he reached the Table Land – a moonscape just above treeline where the Katahdin ridge flattens out considerably. "It was vast, Titanic, and such as man never inhabits. Some part of the beholder; even some vital part, seems to escape through the loose grating of his ribs as he ascends," Thoreau wrote in his account. He had climbed lesser mountains, mostly wooded monadnocks scattered throughout central and southern New England, but this was different. A cloud-covered arctic alpine environment spread in all directions before him, the likes of which he had never seen before. Speaking in the third person about "man" but obviously referring to himself, Thoreau wrote: "Nature has got him at disadvantage, caught him alone, and pilfers him of some of his divine faculty. She does not smile on him as in the plains."

Thoreau did not reach Baxter Peak, the highest point on Katahdin. The rest of the party was somewhere below and out of sight. Concerned that they might leave him behind, he turned back before reaching the top. He had enough food and gear in his pack to make his way back to the river alone, but he did not relish the prospect. He found the rest of his party gathering mountain cranberries right where he'd last seen them. From there, just below the clouds, the wilds of Maine spread before them for a hundred miles – a sea of green broken by countless lakes and ponds cast over the earth like shards of glass, reflecting the blue sky overhead.

Mt. Katahdin has been known for its ferocity since time immemorial. The Penobscots, a branch of the Abenaki people who had lived in the shadow of the mountain long before white men came along, considered Katahdin a dangerous yet sacred place. No doubt the young braves among them must have climbed the mountain on occasion but, generally speaking, the Penobscots tended to avoid that treeless world. Powerful spirits were known to live there – forces that no sensible man or woman ever disturbed. The mountain's most threatening spirit, Pamola, is a man/eagle creature who inhabits the uppermost regions of the mountain during the colder season, along with clouds, fierce winds and snow. Anyone who didn't return from Katahdin was thought to be killed by that demon.

Thursday, Charlie and I rise at dawn, quickly break camp and drive to the trailhead at Roaring Brook Campground. Originally, we had intended to climb Abol Slide as Thoreau did, but a more gradual ascent through the Great Basin on the other side of the mountain seems the better choice. We are signing into the trail register at Roaring Brook Campground a half hour later. It's a beautiful day for a hike. There isn't a cloud anywhere, although the vague threat of rain later in the day has been written on the chalkboard at the ranger's cabin. Temperatures dipped below freezing last night but are in the 40s already. Will probably reach the 50s by this afternoon. Absolutely perfect climbing weather. We shoot up the trail with all due enthusiasm.

We pass a couple disappointed climbing groups on our way up Chimney Pond Trail. They waited two days for the summit of the mountain to clear only to hike away from it this morning. We've been milling about the area all week, so now we're able to take full advantage of this break in the weather. The ring of clouds that commonly clings to the summit has disappeared. We ascend into a clear blue sky feeling blessed.

At Chimney Pond, roughly 2,900 feet above sea level, we take a long break to fortify ourselves with carbohydrates before making the final ascent. There's a thousand-foot wall of grey rock directly in front of us, with sloping conifers at its base and a thin coat of fresh snow on top. Baxter Peak, the highest point on the ridge above us, looks far away and unattainable. But the sign at the trail junction is encouraging, informing us that the peak is only 2.2 miles away via the Saddle Trail. Since the Knife Edge Trail remains closed and the Cathedral Trail is too steep, we head up the Saddle Trail without giving the matter a second thought.

As the trail steepens, the yellow birches and spruce trees around us become stunted and the rock underfoot becomes broken and loose. Somewhere around 3600 feet, we cross our last water source. From there it's a dry scramble over a jumble of rocks and boulders another five or six hundred feet up to a small slide. The slide, just above the treeline, leads to the saddle that happens to be the lowest point on the ridge above. We mount it with steady resolve. The wind blowing up the opposite side of the mountain greets us with an icy embrace as we crest the ridge. We quickly don our jackets and hats. The Table Land stretches before us – scree spreading in all directions. A couple inches of snow has settled over the scree, so footing is precarious. We step gingerly through the rock and ice, following the cairns marking the trail. The summit is still half a mile away.

Over my right shoulder, I can see the top of Abol slide and a trail marking Thoreau's approach. He was wise to turn back when he did. Imagining this rocky wasteland in the clouds with no cairns to follow, I see how he would have been in trouble had he continued. Getting up the mountain would have been easy enough, but going back down the way he came, well, that would have been almost impossible.

There's a ten-foot pile of rocks atop Baxter Peak that marks a point exactly one mile above sea level. Ravens circle the summit as if to warn intruders like us that we have entered a mystical realm. Despite the endless parade of hikers on this mountain, this place is no less hostile than it was in Thoreau's day. We soak in as much of the view as we can before the cold becomes too biting. The icy Knife Edge Trail twists away to the northeast – forbidden fruit. Beyond it, there are lakes and woods all the way to the Canadian horizon. Chimney Pond due north and right below us is merely a puddle. The lesser mountains to the north are too numerous to count. Chesuncook and Moosehead Lakes sprawl in the west. To the south lay Hale Pond, Abol Falls and the Pemadumcook chain of lakes, including Ambajejus, looking placid and somewhat distant.

A chilling wind urges our departure. We congratulate ourselves for having the patience and perseverance to get here, then make a dash for the cover of trees a little over a mile away. Dark clouds approach from the northwest as we hobble through the scree to the saddle. Neither Charlie nor I care to tangle with

Pamola. We are glad to get beneath the treeline before the weather changes.

5

Coming down the mountain, Thoreau and his party followed a rivulet that eventually became Katahdin Stream. They were surprised when they encountered a footprint that could only have been their own. Soon they came to the "Burnt Lands" – a deforested area that had been torched by lightning. "Perhaps I most fully realized that this was primeval, untamed and forever untamable *Nature*, or whatever else men call it, while coming down this part of the mountain," Thoreau wrote. The land wasn't so much charred as it was desolate – an open place in the forest littered with stumps and young poplars. Yet Thoreau was shaken by it. The hand of a fierce god was at work here.

The savage nature of the surrounding forest did not escape Henry David Thoreau's attention during the long descent. "This was that Earth of which we have heard, made of Chaos and Old Night," he wrote years later, "Here was no man's garden, but the unhandselled globe." One can speculate endlessly about how much the landscape has changed since Thoreau's time, but my impression seconds his. I, too, am deeply moved by its primordial ways. Although the Maine Woods isn't the virgin wilderness that it once was, it has retained much of its original character, namely a pervasive rawness.

Despite nearly two centuries of intrusion by the more industrious, beaver-like members of our species, this great northern forest remains harsh yet beautiful – wondrous precisely in its benign indifference to the throng of humanity only a few hundred miles south. A howling wilderness some would call it, but its voice is more like the endless whisper of wind through conifers. Terribly silent, the Maine Woods is a moody universe of dank understory and open water, of shadow and light. The bones and feathers found along a churning stream take on pointed meaning. Here bear, moose and eagle still live at large. Suddenly the observer feels observed. And slowly it becomes apparent that even humankind is not immune to the wiles of that ever-present and all-powerful force called Nature.

Thoreau and his party found their boat late afternoon, shot down the river and portaged Abol Falls, rapidly making their way home. They got as far as Pockwockamus Falls then made camp. The next day they broke camp in haste, slipped down to Ambajejus Lake and across the Pemadumcook Lakes without stopping. They reached Tom Fowler's house that night. And the rest of Thoreau's trip back to Concord was uneventful.

Charlie and I carefully ease down the trail, making sure to avoid a twisted ankle. At Chimney Pond we stop to watch a bull moose and accompanying cow lounging in the brush. With only three hours of daylight left, though, we can't loaf about too much. We resume the hike after slaking our thirst, maintaining a steady clip as we descend.

Tired and footsore, the best part of the hike is behind us now, so it's just a matter of finishing. In one last burst of energy, we charge into Roaring Brook

Campground. We use the remnant twilight to collect water, then cook dinner by lantern. The slightest task requires tremendous effort, but we bask in the glow of triumph, grateful for a clear shot at the summit. After dinner we hit the sack, falling asleep to the sounds of a camp still bustling with activity. I catch a glimpse of the full moon washing through the trees. I would like to stay up and witness the partial lunar eclipse around midnight, but that's simply out of the question. My eyes won't stay open.

To our great surprise, Charlie and I crawl out of bed Friday morning feeling energized. We return to our boat after breaking camp and slip back into the water. In one last hurrah, we paddle across Ambajejus and deep into Pemadumcook Lake, through the Porus Islands. From there it's a somewhat tenuous paddle westward along the shoreline through shallow water, so we stop for a while to rest. Studying the maps, we are tempted to venture farther west to Moose Island and make camp there, but it's too far from the boat launch. We have a long drive home tomorrow, so we backtrack to the spit of land between Pemadumcook and Ambajejus, instead. There we make camp. Night falls upon us with predicable yet awe-inspiring silence.

The next day, a steady southeast wind gives the water a slight chop. We walk the beach for a couple hours, waiting for the wind to subside. It dies down a little by mid-morning so we launch the Klepper, heavily laden with driftwood, and commence the two-mile crossing. A small island off the spit provides shelter from the wind for a short while, but soon enough we are in the broad lake with our bow dipping into the swells as we run towards the distant shore. With the wind at our backs, we make good time. After a half hour of sustained paddling, we are soaking wet but in safe harbor. The Klepper touches land a few minutes later, then it's over. We dismantle the boat, pack up and take to the road. The warm, dry interior of the car seems an unspeakable indulgence.

"What is most striking in the Maine Wilderness is the continuousness of the forest, with fewer open intervals or glades than you had imagined," says Thoreau. My experience doesn't quite bear this out. Maine's vast forest is striking enough, but there is a sense of openness when you are on the water that one rarely experiences back in Vermont woods, where mountains dominate the landscape instead of lakes. Here in Maine, the sandy flats slowly rising out of the ocean collide with the uppermost end of the Appalachians to create a curious mix of dark forest and water awash in sunlight. All the same, there's a wildness here that you don't get elsewhere. Even today, the Maine woods remain heavily logged but not thickly settled, much as it was in Thoreau's time. It is more wilderness than one expects to find in the Northeast.

Expansive wildlands create the conditions for expansive thoughts. No doubt Thoreau's perception of the natural world was greatly influenced by his trips into the Maine Woods. During the latter years of his life, he ventured north two more times and wrote at length about his experiences there. The last two words he uttered on his deathbed were "Moose" and "Indians" – proof positive that his mind was preoccupied with places wilder than his comfortable Concord. The unbroken forest is a powerful teacher, leaving its mark on everyone it touches. And for some people, like Henry David Thoreau and myself, that mark is indelible.

NATURAL CAUSES

For thousands of years philosophers have speculated about what is real, as if reason could do what the five senses cannot. The discussion almost always goes astray, sinking deep into the quagmire of semantics until it all seems like so much frivolous wordplay. But life itself takes center stage in any heartfelt consideration of the matter. And death, of course, is right there with it. Such discussions usually occur indoors, in urban areas, in halls of higher learning where books and papers are the fundamental reality. Yet deep in the nearby forest an unending drama is being played out with all the intensity of creation and apocalypse, undercutting the petty abstractions of the frail human mind. Oddly enough, philosophers like me retreat into the forest to relax, to escape the heaviness of abstract thoughts and simply be in the world for a while. We do not expect to learn anything in the process.

The surrounding trees slowly take shape in the first light of day as I crawl from underneath my tarp. Jesse, a long-haired German Shepherd and faithful companion, follows my lead. She emerges from the same makeshift shelter to yawn, stretch and relieve herself. A quick breakfast then we bushwhack back to the trail a hundred yards away, leaving our camp hidden in the thick brush along Bourn Brook. The trail is shrouded with mist.

Fly rod in hand, I set a brisk pace while moving northward up the trail. Jesse lags behind, temporarily distracted by some irresistible smell. A moment later she bounds ahead of me. For a half hour we travel like that, winding deeper into Vermont's Lye Brook Wilderness. Eventually, a slight elevation change queues me to the small wetland that I'm using as a navigational landmark. I leave the trail, following a compass bearing due east beyond the wetland. Winhall River is half a mile ahead, snaking along the easternmost boundary of the wilderness area. The descent to it is steep so Jesse and I choose our footing carefully. Less than an hour from camp, we reach the fast-moving, amber stream. I pause just long enough on the bank to assemble my fishing gear before stepping into the cool water.

As any seasoned fly fisher will tell you, timing is everything. Last night I enjoyed a busy hour just before dusk, extracting a half dozen small trout from Bourn Brook despite the lingering midsummer heat. This morning I expect even better action. Bigger trout should rise from this substantially larger stream before the sun burns away the thin mist and heats the water enough to stop the ongoing fly hatch. I thread the leader though the guides of my rod with expectant joy. Jesse wades up to her chest in the nearest pool and drinks her fill before breaking into a toothy, water-dripping smile.

A raven calls in the distance – a sure sign that we are in a wild place. The constant rush of clear water over stones soothes the ear. The leaves of birch trees hanging over the stream barely rustle in a faint breath of air. Already yesterday's sweaty, eight-mile trek has been justified by the prevailing forest silence. A slight sprinkle from an overcast sky darkens the stones at my feet, deepening the emerald gleam of the mossy stream bank. A squadron of black flies attacks me while I'm tying a dry fly to my leader, but I don't mind too much. The stream dances before me, its cascading water smelling of ozone, and I am free at last from my own stuffy thoughts.

Fecundity is the first law of nature or so it seems as one meanders through the northern forest. Life is abundant and cheap. Beneath a canopy of leaves thick enough to screen out most daylight, there's a tangle of hobblebush, striped maple and other woody shrubs. Young, slow-growing conifers conspire with the rotting carcasses of fallen trees to make bushwhacking slow and difficult. The forest floor itself is a mosaic of ferns, mosses, lichens and a hundred different flowering plants. There are mushrooms on fallen limbs, chipmunks rummaging amid dead leaves, worms twisting through raw earth and airborne insects everywhere. The natural world is an endless riot of living and dying things, of biomass so thick that there seems no end to it. The swampy, stagnant pools are covered with algae. Fungus grows on every boulder. It is impossible to escape the dank smell of life and death intermingling.

What is real? A deep woods wanderer doesn't bother asking that question. It takes all of one's energy just to keep pace with the highly animated forest. Leave such questions to those who can ponder them in the relative sterility of quiet rooms. This isn't the time or place for idle speculation.

After a full hour of casting, I begin wondering what's wrong. I snatch a mayfly from the air, then match it with one of my artificials. Still no luck. A hundred casts and only one halfhearted rise. Jesse spooks a trout waiting patiently for breakfast in the middle of a pool. Its dark silhouette flashes across the shallow water for an instant before disappearing beneath a half-submerged rock. I spook another one a few minutes later. The fish are here, they just aren't rising. The windless air is thick with wet heat already. Maybe that's the problem. No matter. I keep moving and casting, moving and casting... I'm happy enough simply walking this stream, enjoying the interplay of stone and water at every turn.

But the forest is full of surprises. Just when I have resigned myself to an uneventful morning, I spot something atop a boulder about thirty yards ahead. It seems strangely out of context. Jesse also sees it so I tell her to stay behind me as we approach. Slowly it comes into focus: a rather large bird lying belly down on the gray rock, wings spread apart and face cocked to one side. It's a kingfisher – a fully matured male as big as a woodpecker. It must be dead, I tell myself, but it's eyes open halfway when I prod it with a stick. Then they flutter and close. The kingfisher's beak opens and shuts repeatedly, as if the old bird is trying to tell me something. Suddenly I feel uneasy, like a voyeur caught in the act. So I toss the stick aside and step away.

Despite my self-consciousness, I succumb to curiosity. I go back to the dying bird and carefully inspect it. The kingfisher's plumage has a healthy luster. There is no injury – no blood, loose feathers or broken bones. From all outward appearances, the kingfisher is fine. Mindboggling. I have seen much carnage in the wild. I have witnessed the messy demise of many forest creatures over the years, but never anything like this.

Jesse doesn't even try to figure it out. She simply sees the bird for what it is – a golden opportunity. Jesse creeps in closer, hoping that I'll let her take full advantage of the situation. "No!" I shout at her so she recoils. Then I command her to stay at my side as I gradually draw away from the dying creature. Jesse obeys under protest, emitting a low-pitched groan.

About fifty yards from the kingfisher, I sit down on a rock. From this vantage point the bird is only a tiny blue speck resting motionless on a boulder. I start thinking about an older generation, about relatives living and dead, about my parents – my father in particular. His most recent heart attack has made it clear to me that he won't be around forever. There's absolutely nothing that I can do about it, either. I am a mere observer gazing through the window of time at unalterable events. It is easy to ask, "What is real?" but hard to face up to reality. Life runs its course. Death is final. These simple facts hit me with such force that I can't help but shed a few tears. I am overwhelmed by the starkness of it all, by the horror of unbending truth. Only then does it dawn on me that I've never seen a wild creature die of natural causes. Not until now.

I turn to my faithful companion while wiping away the tears but she's not there. Instead Jesse has crept halfway back to the kingfisher with all the stealth of a bona fide predator. Once again I shout "No!" after her. She veers away from the object of her attention, skulking into the dark shadows of the forest. Jesse knows that I mean business but there is something else driving her, something that runs deeper than the bond between us. A few yards downstream of the kingfisher, she emerges from the forest. Silhouetted in a sudden blaze of morning light, Jesse looks more wolfish and menacing than I've ever seen her look before. So I get up and walk back to the bird as if to claim it. Jesse relents and the contest is over, just like that. We continue upstream, around the bend and out of sight -- a fly rod whipping the air and a canine looking for brand new opportunities.

One more hour of practice casting then I quit the stream. Jesse stays close to me as we bushwhack through a dense stand of spruce on a shortcut back to the trail. We play together in a forest clearing to partially erase from memory that incident on the stream. Then we return to our camp along Bourn Brook. Later on I gather up my things and move south to Bourn Pond where the fecundity of the forest gives way to open water, air and light. There we are greeted by a loon. Its cry echoes across the pond as if to assure me that I've made the right decision.

Natural causes? It is no more practical to dissect that term than it is to ponder reality. The wild has its way of rendering such notions absurd, of making it clear that the world cannot be grasped by reason alone. So I fix dinner for Jesse and myself from the dried provisions I've brought with me, quite satisfied to forego the taste of fresh fish. Then we sit together by the pond at dusk – a philosopher and his dog watching trout rise and mosquitoes buzz as the last threads of light fade away. The loon swims about nonchalantly, occasionally diving for its dinner. An owl hooting in the distance keeps me from drifting too far into my abstractions. And life is good.

CHILI DOGS
ON MOUNT WASHINGTON

Even though the forest shade moderates the midsummer heat, I am sweating profusely only minutes out of the Route 2 parking lot. My backpacking companion, John, is also sweating – just not as heavily. He's in better shape than me. I have Vermont legs while John's a flatlander from Ohio, but he's been jogging daily for months so he's more ready for this trek than I am. His breaths are measured despite the fifty-pound packs we both carry. I'm gasping for air, all too aware of the sedentary life I've been living the past few years. A half mile up the web of trails on the northern slope of the Presidential Range, I have to stop and rest. My heart feels like it's about to leap right out of my chest. While I wait for it to settle down, I seriously question the wisdom of this four-day outing.

Five hours, four miles and 3,000 vertical feet later, John and I approach the shelter where we'll spend the night. It's called The Perch and rightly so, being a niche carved out of the side of the mountain like an afterthought. I whip a small rock into the air and watch it arc slowly before dropping into the trees a thousand feet below. This isn't the kind of place my acrophobic wife would like, that's for sure. But I revel in the altitude, giddy with the prospect of being so high in the White Mountains. With the kind of pragmatism that comes naturally to most engineers, John fires up his stove and immediately sets to work on dinner. I stumble down the path to a trickle in the rocks to refill water bottles. There I silently give thanks to water – the magical substance that got me up here despite my rather flaccid physique.

In the morning, shortly after breaking camp, we climb above the treeline. We enter a moonscape of lichen-covered granite – the vast expanse of arctic/alpine scree that practically defines New Hampshire's Presidential Range. Nowhere else east of the Mississippi can one enjoy 360-degree views while trekking above treeline all day long. Beneath a partly cloudy sky, I'm all jazzed up and chattering nonstop like a radio commentator. John stoically endures my blather, no doubt considering it the price he must pay to hike these mountains with me. On the other side of Edmunds Col, halfway up the rock pile known as Mt. Jefferson, I recall something Lao Tzu once said: "To be always talking is against nature." With that in mind, I shut my trap and try to hike the rest of the day with the reverence that the surrounding wild country deserves.

Atop Mt. Jefferson, I calm down enough to actually enjoy our small achievement as a cool breeze blows up the mountainside. Remarkably, we have the summit to ourselves. A half dozen other hiking parties are visible in the distance but they're all too far away to matter. When finally a pair of hikers joins us, we relinquish the peak. Then we turn our thoughts to the day's main event: Mount Washington. It looms before us – a great dome of rock partly shrouded by clouds, rising another thousand feet, at least, above the saddle into which we're descending.

Now comes the big push. We brace ourselves for it by setting a steady, rhythmic pace. My walking stick clicks against the rocks as I probe the trail with it like a blind man, feeling for solid footing amid the scree. Conversation falls off to nothing as we both slip into that sense of immediacy familiar to all mountaineers, where mind, body and spirit fuse. As the contemplative climber Robert Leonard Reid wrote in *The Great Blue Dream*: "Mystic and mountaineer alike move heavenward through the practice of the ascetic arts: austerity, endurance, denial." Yeah, guys like John and me live for this kind of thing – for the rawness of nature, its wild beauty and our corporeal selves pushed to the limit by it. This is nothing less than a dance with the sublime. Mount Washington in all its magnificence, the highest and most formidable mountain in the Northeast, does not disappoint in this regard.

To conserve energy, we detour around a lesser summit, Mt. Clay, though it rises tantalizingly nearby. The top of Mt. Washington won't be the end of the line for us. By dusk we'll be thousands of feet below it, camped somewhere in the Great Gulf. So we must conserve our strength, refrain from acting upon impulse. Nothing is more important in mountaineering than foresight. Without it, an excursion into alpine regions can quickly turn sour. On this count, John and I both agree.

Right after skirting Mt. Clay and passing the Jewell Trail that rises abruptly out of the western valley, we encounter some hut-to-hut hikers, then a few day hikers, then a few more. A pair of pubescent girls wearing tennis shoes, cotton shorts and skimpy blouses dart past. Their grinning parents amble along ten minutes later. The uppermost portion of Mt. Washington comes into full view as the trail sweeps to the southeast. The mountain looks something like an anthill with so many bright specs moving all over it. Then I spot something I've never seen in all my years of mountaineering: a rail line below and to our right, rising to the summit above. For a second I wonder if perhaps I'm imagining things. Then a whistle blows.

The Cog Railway rises 3,600 feet from the Marshfield Station to the summit of Mount Washington – an engineering feat for its time, to be sure. Back in 1852, a meatpacking baron named Sylvester Marsh dreamt up the idea of mechanized access to New Hampshire's highest mountain. By 1869, despite the dour predictions of naysayers, he completed it. Now a steam-driven locomotive muscles its way up the mountain along a cog railway, pushing two cars full of people. John and I stop halfway up the rocky slope of Mt. Washington to catch our breath, watching the train clatter past slowly, spewing a plume of black smoke all the way. It's as if we've stepped back into time. Tourists sitting placidly on the train snap pictures of us, as if we're part of the fauna promised in the brochure. Once the train has passed, we cross the cinder-laden track and finish our assault on the mountain. Just above, a concrete bunker and several smaller buildings taunt us with their relative proximity. We're almost there.

A hard half-hour later, John and I struggle onto the summit. Flush with victory, we drop our packs and guzzle down water. Slowly the lightheadedness subsides. Standing in a throng of tourists now, we patiently wait our turn to set foot on the actual highest point of the mountain. There we have our picture taken by a jovial fellow, in exchange for taking his. Despite the haze of exhaustion, I see John and myself through the eyes of those who have come here by cog railway or the long, winding auto road: we're two sweaty, dirty backpackers looking a little out of place. Amid the welter of people moving in and out of the Sherman Adams Summit Building, there are plenty of hikers like us taking care of their needs: filling water bottles from the outdoor faucet, using the toilet or simply resting up. But very few of them are hauling around huge packs like ours.

Mount Washington, they say, is home to the world's worst weather. With three major storm tracks converging on it, a summit in the clouds two-thirds of the time and hurricane-force winds blowing up it a hundred days per year, the mountain is a challenge to even the most seasoned hikers. It has a couple thousand feet of rock protruding above treeline, so there's nowhere to hide when the weather suddenly turns bad, as it does on a fairly regular basis. 124 people have died on or around Mt. Washington since 1849. Since a quarter million people visit this mountain annually, it's a wonder that the body count isn't higher. Highest wind recorded here: 231 miles per hour. Lowest temperature: -47 degrees Fahrenheit. And wind chill off the charts. A dozen people have died of hypothermia on Mt. Washington *during the summer months*. The mountain has a wicked temper, yet most people coming here are oblivious to it – walking around its summit as if they were strolling through a city park.

Inside the Summit Building, John and I discover a food court. Though we're carrying plenty of food, we can't resist the convenience. Digging deep into our packs, we produce money for some fast food. Lunch is a couple chili dogs, a bag of chips and soda. Good junk. John takes a picture of me hoisting my chili dog – proof that it really did happen this way. For reasons that defy logic, I am tempted to wander into the gift shop and look at stuff. John suggests that we fill our water bottles and get going before the weather turns. That is certainly the prudent thing to do.

  The train passes us as we step gingerly through the scree, backtracking a quarter mile down to a trail junction. There we pick up the Great Gulf Trail, which drops rapidly to Spaulding Lake beneath the treeline. The descent takes a couple hours to negotiate, even though the lake isn't much more than a mile away as the crow flies. We take a well-deserved break there, then trace the headwaters of the West Branch Peabody River down deeper into the forested wilderness. The acrid scent of the coal smoke lingers in the valley even when the train whistle is no longer audible. We try to ignore the smell as we follow the cascading stream, looking for a good place to camp. "No camping" signs confound us for the next mile. Eventually we get beyond them, finding a nice piece of flat ground tucked into the conifers not far from the water. There we set up tarp and tent, then collapse.

Third day out, we climb up the Buttress Trail, getting back above the treeline by mid-afternoon like the crazy, forty-something Boy Scouts that we are. The evening before, I thought I might have to limp down the valley to the nearest road, but a good night's sleep has revitalized me. John is always ready to bag another peak, so he's glad to see me rally. We huff and puff over the shoulder of Mt. Adams, northward and upward until we reach Madison Hut in the saddle between Mt. Adams and Mt. Madison. There I rest, guarding the packs, while John hikes up Mt. Adams and back. Afterward we both hobble down to the Valley Way Tent site on the northern slope, just below treeline, to spend the night. No doubt our combined snoring keeps some wild animals awake all night.

The last day is an easy descent back to the trailhead parking lot. I'm animated and yapping again, happy to have survived the trek: 7,700 feet vertical, 21 miles and many hours of hard hiking. Not bad for a couple of middle-aged backpackers. What'll we do next year? I suggest a long, easy meander through a relatively flat forest – something off the beaten path, a little less accessible. Something more like a wilderness experience. The chili dogs were tasty, but not what I'm after when I venture into the great outdoors.

PILGRIMAGE TO LOST POND

1

Right after the road changes from pavement to dirt, I spot something moving through the woods to my left. A deer drifts through a sunny glade, then slips back into forest shadows. I slam on the brakes. A cloud of dust envelops my old pickup truck. I snap my fingers to get the attention of the German shepherd dog sitting next to me, but she's too busy sniffing the air – head out the passenger window. By the time Jesse turns her head towards me, the deer has disappeared into the foliage. No matter. Spotting the deer is a good omen. I step on the accelerator, finishing the ten-mile drive from the main highway to Wakely Dam. Just beyond the dam, another mile and a half up the narrowing road, I find a turnout next to an easily overlooked trailhead. There I leave the truck and commence a weeklong trek, hiking southward into one of the largest roadless areas in the Adirondacks: the West Canada Lakes Wilderness.

My pack is heavy but I don't care. I've waited two years for this moment – it taking that long for me to break out of my regular routine. With walking stick firmly in hand, I charge down the trail. Jesse falls behind immediately. Old dog on her last leg, she's been having a hard time keeping up with me lately. The heat of a sultry August afternoon doesn't help matters. So I cut my pace to match hers. This could very well be Jesse's last big outing. I want to make sure that it's a good one for her.

A half hour into the hike, I stop at a campsite on the Cedar River Flow. The Flow is a long, shallow body of water created by Wakely Dam a few miles north. Deer flies have been chewing up Jesse's ears worse than usual so I apply some bug dope to them. Afterwards, I walk down to the water's edge for a good look at the reedy lake. Jesse wades a few yards out to soak her belly while gulping down the cool, clear water – her long-haired coat holds the heat. A solitary loon calls in the distance, as if to welcome me and my four-legged companion to the wild. And the stress of the four-hour drive from home to trailhead this morning quickly dissipates.

West Canada Lake is roughly fifteen miles from the trailhead. It's located right in the middle of a sprawling forest. With a good path underfoot, I could easily reach it in two days. But taking my dog's poor health into consideration, I think I'll do it in three. There's no rush. I have eight days to get there and back, doing whatever comes naturally in the process. I've done enough backpacking to know how to get the most out of an outing. My hardcore trekking days are behind me. Since hiking Vermont's Long Trail end-to-end several years back, I've had a change of heart. Now it's all about being in the woods, not just passing through them.

The Northville/Lake Placid Trail is fairly well marked and easy to follow despite being overgrown in places. It isn't used much, compared to that network of cattle-paths crisscrossing the High Peaks. There aren't many 4,000-foot peaks located near this meandering, 130-mile trail and that, I suppose, is what keeps it from being overrun. The Northville/Lake Placid Trail begins in the southwestern corner of the Adirondack Park, winds northward through boggy, relatively flat country before turning slightly east at Long Lake. From there the trail cuts along the western edge of the High Peaks to Lake Placid. There are plenty of lakes and ponds along the way. That's the main reason I'm on it. I want to ply backcountry waters for trout while enjoying Adirondack wildness. I have a fly rod as well as a compass and intend to put both to good use.

Closed gentian and meadowsweet grow in abundance along the trail as it passes through shady forest groves and patches of sun-drenched grass. Here the Northville/Lake Placid Trail follows an old woods road. But the double track, wide enough to accommodate a jeep, disappears into a large wetland. On the other side of the wetland, a narrower path emerges. And trail markers appear more frequently. The heart of the wilderness can't be far away.

Not too far south of the wetland, I stumble into a trail junction. Turning down the side trail, I quickly reach the Cedar River Lean-To. Is the day's hike over already? Four miles isn't much of a trek, but it's enough for my dog the first day out. A family of canoeists paddle away just as Jesse and I appear in front of the shelter. I drop my pack and immediately start cleaning up the place. The shelter is full of brush. Half-charred pieces of green wood litter the ground all around the fire pit. Jesse goes down to the river to cool off. Returning to camp, she collapses into the grass on the shady side of the shelter to watch me putter. I use a dull, rusty axe left at the shelter to split up the pieces of charred wood so they'll burn better.

One full hour of late-afternoon solitude, then I'm joined by three tired thru-hikers. They're doing the Northville/Lake Placid Trail end-to-end, from south to north. Oddly enough, the oldest of the three – a slender man in his 60s – is the least experienced. His son, Mark, has introduced him to backpacking. The third fellow, Jeff, is a thirty-something athlete who hooked up with them along the way. I push my things into a corner of the shelter, making room for them. They use that space to stash some of their gear, then set up tents in tall grass. The untrammeled ground is softer there.

The older man, Fred, is a retired engineer. His son is a businessman. Jeff teaches grade school. And what do I do? I'm reluctant to say since my vocation has been something of a sore spot with me lately. "I'm a writer," I mutter, "But not a particularly successful one." Jeff asks why. Surprising myself, I blurt out the cold, hard truth of it: "I'm too much the philosopher and not enough of a wordsmith." As luck would have it, Jeff studied a lot of philosophy back in college so this disclosure excites him. He starts dropping "-Isms" all over the place, trying to pin one on me. From the way he fields provocative statements, I can tell that he's aching for a philosophical argument – the kind that people win or lose like boxing matches. I don't rise to his challenge at first, but eventually his rather casual comments about man and nature set me off. And before anyone is ready for it, I'm on a two-minute tirade about the authenticity of the wild and the absurdity of civilization.

"No, seriously now. Tell us what you *really* think," Fred says, trying to interject a little levity into the conversation. Jeff ignores the queue. Instead the young schoolteacher gives us all a lecture on the evils of technology as he fires up his camp stove. Dinnertime. I know better than to ruin a perfectly good meal with this kind of talk but can't help myself. I tell Jeff that I'm reluctant to discard tools – things such as knives, cooking pots and firestarters – that have proven to be so useful over the millennia.

"Sounds like you want it both ways," Jeff concludes, rather frustrated now by what he perceives as my evasiveness.

"I just don't buy into tidy, anti-technology credos, that's all," I respond, adding that I don't see any need for credos or the gurus who push them. Jeff is alarmed by this proclamation and I really should drop the matter, but I feel compelled to deliver a finishing blow: "Jesse is all the guru I need."

Am I joking? All three of the tired hikers stop what their doing and stare at me. The conversation is now in danger of really turning sour, so Jeff and I tacitly agree to change the subject. We start talking about food bartering on the trail, the trials and tribulations of thru-hiking – safe stuff like that. And the rest of the dinner hour is a much more pleasant affair.

After dinner, I grab my fly rod and go down to the river. I rig up while standing along the river's edge. Jesse joins me, finding a nice spot in the cool mud to lie down and watch. Some mayflies hatch at dusk and a few fish rise to the dimpled surface, but I hook nothing. The fierce assaults of no-see-ums and mosquitoes make it difficult to concentrate. Or perhaps I'm still too upset about that dinnertime outburst of mine to focus upon what I'm doing. Either way, my fly casting is fruitless.

For several months now, I've been trying to work up the courage to commit my worldview to paper. I feel a strong urge to write down my deepest thoughts on God, nature and humankind, but am convinced from the poor showing of my previous "think" pieces that no one wants to read stuff like that. In fact, I'm convinced that the best way to sink my already foundering literary career is to spout ideas that are neither popular nor easy to understand. I envy those with philosophies that are taken seriously – I've never been so fortunate. I despise those who tell others only what they want to hear; yet I see the practicality in it. Where does that leave me? Having to choose between intellectual dishonesty and literary suicide. Not the best place to be.

I glance at the clouds gathering along the dark horizon, wondering if it's going to rain tonight. Then I look over to my dog tucked into the riverbank. She raises her head to a distant rumble; I do the same. It's true, really. I didn't just say it to spike the conversation. Jesse *is* my guru, reminding me daily about the importance of being in the moment. Whenever I start getting too bogged down in my own abstractions, she's there to set me right. But society doesn't put much credence in the wisdom of dogs or rants of backwoods philosophers, so now what? Backpack and fly rod come in handy whenever the tension between me and my fellowman gets to be too much. These leisure tools help me get away, anyhow. But the wild itself is a constant reminder that I can't censor myself indefinitely about matters of ultimate concern. It's a paradox to be sure.

2

A gentle rain fell overnight as thunderstorms rolled through the region. Yesterday's heat has given way to morning coolness. Jesse is invigorated by it. She jumps to her feet and starts chasing her tail in an unexpected display of enthusiasm. I put an end to a long, lazy breakfast routine and start packing. My camp companions, slow to rise and get going, are now at it as well. A few minutes later they are back on the trail, headed north. Shortly thereafter, Jesse and I are southbound.

Today we're going as far as Cedar Lakes, about five miles away. The Northville/Lake Placid Trail climbs over the shoulder of Lamphere Ridge, then drops into a narrow valley. It's pretty easy going – road grade most of the way. All the same, the trail has a wilder feel to it now, twisting and turning through the trees, around rocks, over exposed roots and across muddy little bogs. Jesse's out front at first, but soon falls behind me. In trail-pounding mode now, a habit developed during my month-long trek on the Long Trail, I'm moving a bit too fast for her. So I stop and drop my pack when the trail reaches the valley stream. That gives Jesse time enough to slake her thirst. She wades into the middle of the stream. Here the Cedar River is a mountain brook: cold, clear, shallow, about ten yards wide. It has an amber hue to it as most Adirondack streams do, but is clean enough to hold trout. I consider breaking out my rod and testing its waters, but no, I'm in hiking mode now. So then, after sharing a handful of peanuts with Jesse, I return to trail-pounding.

The trail climbs back up the Lamphere Ridge, even though my map shows it hugging the stream. Hmm, that's a serious discrepancy. I check my compass as a precaution before going any farther. Decades of backcountry travel have taught me never to completely trust trails. More than once, I've followed well-beaten paths into oblivion.

Around noon, Jesse and I drag our feet into a clearing next to Cedar Lake, where a lean-to offers some shelter from a thin drizzle. Two slender, thirty-ish women are hanging out at the lean-to. They have no overnight gear, though. This puzzles me. A ribbon of smoke coils from the fire pit – their way of keeping the bugs at bay. We chat a bit. I learn that they've just day hiked here using a side trail from the east, after leaving their car near Pillsbury Mountain. That's surprising. My map shows that trailhead four miles farther east, at Perkins Clearing. That means Cedar Lake is more accessible than I thought. That means there will be other people here.

Another mile down the trail, I cross a footbridge between a shallow body of water called Beaver Pond and the much larger Cedar Lake. Just past the footbridge, a narrow path appears on the left. No sign indicating a shelter that direction, so I keep to the main trail. After a steady, quarter-mile climb, I realize my mistake and retrace my steps back to the unmarked path. Sure enough, there's a shelter a hundred yards down it, occupied by a couple middle-aged canoeists and their two sons. Not wanting to impose myself on them yet in no mood to continue hiking, I follow the narrowing footpath beyond the shelter, skirting the shoreline. About fifty yards away, I find an old fire circle on a patch of flat, open ground among the trees. This will do. I pitch my tarp beneath an old beech to make the place my own.

Completely exhausted, Jesse collapses onto the forest floor. She doesn't move for hours, not even when a bold chipmunk scurries through camp. Poor dog. I pushed her hard today. Pushed myself, too, it seems. There are several hot spots on my feet and one rather large blister on my right heel. Guess the insoles of my boots have broken down more than I thought. Oh well. After setting up camp, I join Jesse for a long, mid-afternoon nap.

An hour or so later, I awaken to the all-too-familiar sound of rustling leaves. Looking over, I spot that pesky chipmunk helping itself to the food bag that I've carelessly left on the ground. I order Jesse to chase the intruder out of camp, but she only stares at the chipmunk, then at me, as if to say she hasn't the energy for it. Exasperated, I fling a stick at our unwelcome guest. That spooks the critter for a while, but ten minutes later it's creeping back into camp again. Finally, I get up and hoist the food bag into the air about eight feet or so, using a cord slung over an overhanging tree branch. And that settles the matter.

Loons call out. I grab my fly rod and scramble down the steep bank to the water's edge to see what's going on. Jesse follows. Several loons bob along the choppy surface, about a quarter mile out. Cedar Lake is big by backcountry standards: several miles long and nearly a mile wide in places. Remarkably pristine. A few shelters dot its shoreline, otherwise there are no manmade structures. Some canoeists are fishing in the middle of the lake – my next-door neighbors, I think. Aside from them, there's no one in sight. Nothing but Adirondack wildness for as far as the eye can see. Pillsbury Mountain rises a few miles beyond the opposite shore. What else? Lots of hemlocks, birches and maples along the rocky shoreline. Few cedars, despite the lake's name. Clouds gather around the mountain. A strong southerly wind gives the lake a gray chop. The loons don't seem to care.

Breaking out my rod, I ply the roily water for trout. Jesse watches from a sandy spot along the rocky shore. Slowly, almost without realizing it, I slip into a funk. The fish aren't biting but that's not the issue. I'm troubled by something else – by some vague longing, an indistinct hunger for god-only-knows-what. My mood defies the lake's beauty and serenity. I don't understand it. I'm so disturbed by the incongruity between my mood and the surrounding landscape that I quit fishing shortly after starting, then go directly back to camp to fix dinner.

Our dinner routine has become rather elaborate recently. First I reconstitute dried milk, then mix Jesse's enzyme powder into it – a rather dubious substitute for her failing pancreas. While the enzymes are activating, I get my own meal going. Fifteen minutes later, I shove several different pills down Jesse's throat – a witches brew of antibiotics and steroids – then add a ration of dried dog food to the brownish, frothing milk. Jesse eats slowly but devours every kibble. She used to be as fussy as a cat about food. Not any more. The steroids make her ravenous. Afterward, she drifts to the edge of camp, finding a nice, soft place in the forest duff to rest. I start a fire and boil up water for ramen and tea. My small fire burns smokeless in the fading light. I check on Jesse every once in a while just to make sure she hasn't wandered into the darkening woods. Not that she would. She's a frail old dog and the forest has teeth, so she stays close to camp.

Twilight lingers. I think about my wife, Judy, and how much she would like this place. Judy loves clear, backcountry lakes and ponds. But I'm out here by myself right now and that's for the best. Married to me over a dozen years, she knows all too well how much I need a solitary excursion into deep woods every once in a while to maintain my sanity. Still, it gets harder and harder to go be out here for extended periods of time without her. The last time I was on the Northville/Lake Placid Trail, she was with me. We enjoyed a lazy week in the woods just north of Duck Hole. Nothing remarkable happened on that trip and that's precisely what made it such a great outing. We spent more time lounging next to a mountain stream than anything else. Yeah, she would like it here. She and Jesse would spend an entire day just swimming about and watching loons, as they have before.

Twilight becomes darkness. Tea cup empty and I've burned most of the wood gathered before dinner. But I'm still in a funk and not sure why. As the bright orange tongues of fire lick back the night, I search them for some insight into myself or the world at large.

Nothing emerges from the flames. Patience, patience. Another day or two out here and the wild will draw it out of me, as it has before. It always does. That's the main reason I come out here, isn't it? Spiritual housecleaning. Time alone in the woods forces everything to the surface.

Big day tomorrow. I secure camp against rain while letting the fire burn down to cooling embers. I call in Jesse who's standing guard about ten yards out. I direct her to a nice cushy spot next to me beneath the tarp. We both need a good night's rest. Tomorrow we're headed for West Canada Lake, five miles farther down the trail. After two years of daydreaming about the place, I'll finally get to see it. Looking forward to that.

3

Wednesday, August 7th. Third day in the woods. I roll out of my warm, dry sleeping bag and into a cool, damp camp. A light rain has soaked everything. Fortunately, I had the foresight to cover a small pile of sticks with a piece of plastic before going to bed, so starting a fire this morning isn't a problem. I pull down the food bag and start breakfast. Jesse wanders away for a quick pee, then drops onto a patch of grass next to the trail to watch the lake. Before the fire burns clean, I consider changing my hiking plans. During a brief encounter with a thru-hiker yesterday afternoon, I learned that several groups are camped at West Canada Lake. I vaguely recall passing a side-trail pointing northwest, about halfway between here and that first lean-to a mile back. Saw a makeshift sign at that trail junction, I think, with the words "Lost Pond" scrawled on it. Can't help but wonder what's up that way. Maybe it's time to leave the beaten path. Hmm. Will have to give the matter more thought later on.

After breakfast, as the campfire embers cool, I sip coffee while poring over my maps. It doesn't take long to find the trail connecting Cedar Lake to Lost Pond and to devise a rather circuitous route north/northeast, back towards Cedar Flow. Taking that route will shorten this outing by ten miles, making things a bit easier for Jesse. Would get me into wilder country, as well. But that would mean abandoning my trek to West Canada Lake. How important is it to reach that body of water? Not nearly as important as shaking off the funk that's been hounding me lately. I really need to spend some time alone in *deep* woods. Lost Pond looks like just the place to do that. It's out of the way, to be sure. Not much reason for anyone to go there. Might even get lucky and have it entirely to myself for a couple days. Wouldn't that be something. A shortened trek would mean that Jesse and I could hang out another day here at Cedar Lake, as well. She could certainly use the down time. Speaking of which... where'd she go?

Walking over to where Jesse had been resting, I look over the steep bank to find her lying in the sand next to the lake. I snuff out my fire, grab my rod and join my lazy dog. It's a calm, quiet, partly cloudy day. The lake's surface is still. No fly hatch. Not the best conditions for fly fishing, but I don't care. I cast my line repeatedly, letting my thoughts sink deep into the lake with my wet fly. Directly across the lake, several loons kick up a racket in a place appropriately called Noisey Inlet. Their haunting calls echo off Pillsbury Mountain. The clouds clinging to the mountain make it appear bigger than it really is. Canoeists floating in the middle of the lake are also trying to fish. Jesse catches a scent in the air. I can only guess what it is. And hours slip away effortlessly.

Late afternoon. I'd be hard-pressed to say what I've done today. Washed a few clothes, sketched, napped, walked over to the nearby Beaver Pond to check it out – what else? After swimming naked in the heat of the day, I stretched across a boulder to watch clouds drift past for a while. A wood duck stopped by for a visit, then a raven. Following Jesse's lead, I've been doing a lot of nothing. Radical deceleration. Can't say that I'm completely in tune with the wild, but I have slowed down enough to notice things I wouldn't have noticed before. Like the way the lake changes its mood during the course of the day, for instance, and how that changes me.

Early evening, I get serious about fishing. A few mayflies appeared on the water just as I was finishing dinner, so now I'm throwing a #18 Adams dry fly out there to float among them. The occasional surface splash gets me going. I pay close attention, keeping my line tight and watching the water intently. Soon enough, wild trout attack my offering. Several near misses, then I hook one. A short fight brings a nine-inch brookie to the shore's rocky edge where it works itself loose. Close enough. Jesse and I both get a good look at it. I cast again. More flies hatch, more splashes, more action at the end of my line as the daylong breeze gives way to dusky stillness. Jesse wades chest-deep in the lake to do a little fishing of her own. At one point, she chases a fish that I've hooked into the shallows where my line wraps around a rock then snaps. I laugh, then tie on another fly with some difficulty, holding it up to the sunset's afterglow. Now my fly is almost impossible to find floating in the dark, watery void. When finally the bats come out, the fish go into a feeding frenzy. But it's too dark to see anything at all. I'm done. I return to camp empty-handed yet happy to call it a day.

Thursday morning, I'm awakened by the persistent knocking of a woodpecker. Slept well last night, lulled into the land of dreams by a great horned owl. Down by the lake, I splash cold water into my face while listening to a solitary loon in Noisey Inlet. The sun peeks through the trees, then burns a hole in the clear blue sky just left of Pillsbury Mountain. A thin mist rises from the glassy lake. The day couldn't be any more promising. Jesse feels the same way I do, breaking into a big smile as she scans the lake and sniffs the air. We exchange knowing looks before returning to camp.

Jesse slips into play mode after breakfast, excitedly chasing her tail like a young pup. I take my time breaking camp, savoring the comfortable familiarity of the place. Lost Pond is only three miles north so there's no need to rush. All the same, I'm eager to hit the trail and get going. Forty-four hours is long enough to stay in one place. Both Jesse and I are in the mood to move.

I drop a handful of nuts near the campfire circle for that chipmunk bandit to enjoy, then brush the ground with a spruce bough to give the site a less-beaten look. One last look around, then I hoist the backpack to my shoulders and go. Jesse's already on the trail.

Backtracking a half-mile, across the footbridge then turning away from Cedar Lake, I find the sketchy side trail that I'd largely ignored the day before yesterday. Sure enough, there's a sign at the trail junction with the words "Lost Pond" etched on it. The narrow path is barely worn yet well marked by yellow discs. Goodbye Northville/Lake Placid Trail, hello deep woods! I tap my walking stick against a birch tree a couple times for good luck, then head north.

Deer tracks and a couple sets of boot prints – I'm not the first one to travel this way. Hope no one's camped at Lost Pond. If so, I'll keep going until I reach Little Moose Lake a bit farther north. I'm flexible. The thin layer of soil underfoot leads me to believe that very few people ever use this trail. Winding through the forest this way and that, it looks as if the person who blazed this trail became disoriented. Not a very direct path, that's for sure. But pleasant all the same. The trail skirts the wetlands of Beaver Pond, that's the main thing. Then it rises out of the lowlands after crossing the pond's outlet and tags an abandoned logging road. Couldn't be easier walking, even though there's a steady uphill climb for half a mile. Sweating and a bit winded after cresting the shoulder of a small mountain, I stop to catch my breath. Jesse looks like she could use a little rest, too.

I study the surrounding forest while sucking down water and munching some trail mix. The tightly knit birches and spruces down by Beaver Pond are gone now. The surrounding woods are bright and airy. Mostly beeches. A good number of them have claw marks in their bark. Jesse sniffs a pile of fresh scat, then knits her brows. "That's right," I respond with a laugh, "This is bear country." Jesse doesn't like it. I produce a couple dog biscuits to take her mind off the troubling discovery, but she clings to my side when we get going again. Sick old dog in the wild – yeah, she's a target all right. But I assure her with a neck rub that everything's going to be okay, that I won't abandon her.

What a beautiful stretch of wild forest! What a glorious day! And drifting slowly along the old woods road couldn't be any easier. Shafts of light break through the green canopy, illuminating the forest. The boot prints have disappeared for one reason or another, so now these woods are all mine. Yessir, this is what it's all about. Glad I left the main trail. Can't wait to see Lost Pond. Will probably have it all to myself. Wonder if there are any trout in it. I beam a big smile at Jesse but she still looks worried. "For Chrissakes, Jes, the bears aren't going to get you," I snap at her. Then I start humming a tune. Not going to let my worrisome dog spoil the moment.

4

When the trail suddenly descends after turning sharply to the east, I stop to check my map and compass. Something's not right. It's supposed to follow the contours westward for a while. Why are the yellow discs taking me some other direction? Either the trail has been rerouted recently or my map's wrong. Hmm. Not one to turn back and not in the mood to leave the trail just yet, I stay with the yellow markers. Guess I'm trusting them now.

The trail drops fast, leveling out just before reaching a small wetland. Next thing I know, the trail markers are running across the top of a beaver dam. Is this some kind of joke? Blindly following the markers, I step gingerly across the tangle of sticks and grass, trying to keep my boots dry. Jesse has more trouble crossing the dam than I do, slipping into the muck a couple times. Somewhat relieved to reach the tall grass on the other side of the dam, I temporarily lose sight of the yellow discs. But they reappear once my feet tag high ground again. When the trail slips into a copse of shadowy conifers, markers become few and far between. I suspect that the narrow path underfoot wouldn't even exist, if it weren't for deer. There's no indication that anyone else has come this way in a while.

After bearing right for a quarter mile, I come to a sign in the middle of nowhere: "Lost Pond .8 mile." An arrow on the sign points sharply to my right, leading me to believe that I'm walking in circles. A quick glance at my compass verifies this. Completely disoriented now, I follow the yellow markers as they weave in and out of the trees. What was once a track cutting through the dense forest is now a series of mud holes. Jesse follows, assuming that I know where I'm going. Shortly after losing the yellow discs, I catch a little light through the trees. Lost Pond, I presume.

Appropriately named, that's for sure. I have only a vague idea where I am right now.

Stepping into the open, first thing I notice is that the pond is entirely surrounded by sphagnum moss. It's a shallow body of water in the middle of what would otherwise be a large bog. No easy access. I drop my pack and walk to the edge of the turf to test its stability. Jesse bounds ahead of me. "No!" I yell, but it's too late. Before the sound of my voice has stopped echoing through the surrounding hills, she's chest deep in muck. I lean over and grab Jesse by the collar as she scrambles back onto the turf. Great. Now the lower half of her body is covered with black mud. Swamp dog. How am I going to clean her up? I look around for a feeder stream but see nothing but timber and turf.

Just then the middle of the pond erupts. I look over to see a huge trout leap two feet into the air, then splash back into the drink. Shock waves ripple across the water's surface, all the way to the distant beaver dam. The fly fisher in me stirs to action, but there's no wading across the pond's mucky bottom and from here I can't cast that far enough to be effective. Damn!

Lost Pond has an utterly wild, almost spooky feeling to it. I'd like to stay here and groove on it for a while but there's nowhere to camp. Nothing but sphagnum moss and thick black spruce in all directions. The sun is high in the sky now and the temperature is climbing. I'm thirsty. My bottles are nearly empty and there's no good water source at hand. The pond is the color of dark ale. Meanwhile, I've got a muck-covered dog to contend with. Fact is, I can't stay here. I've got to find a relatively clean stream.

One last look at the remote pond, reminiscent of other wild places I've been, then I turn away. Now what? Whipping out my map, I study the contours and make an educated guess as to where I'm likely to find a trickle of clear water. More importantly, where am I and how do I get out of here? According to my map, I went through a trail junction about half a mile back. At that sign perhaps? Back there I should find a path connecting Lost Pond Trail to a woods road leading to Little Moose Lake. Surely I'll find some kind of feeder stream along the way. So then, without further hesitation, I shoulder my pack and get going. Swamp dog is right on my heels.

Backtracking to the "Lost Pond" sign is easy. Finding the connector trail isn't. After looking around a minute or two, I find the trail hidden behind the thick branches of a fallen hemlock. Not much of a trail, really, but the yellow disc that I spot on it assures me that it'll take me where I want to go. I step around the fallen hemlock then walk down the trail. And there it is – a feeder stream! Putting my water filter to good use, I slake my thirst while filling both bottles. Then I clean up Jesse. But the ankle-deep rivulet clouds up right away. And a swarm of mosquitoes urges me to get going long before I can wash all the muck out of Jesse's fur.

Now then, to reach that woods road... After following the feeder stream another fifty-yards, the connector trail crosses it. But there's no semblance of a path on the other side. What just happened? I backtrack, look around, go this way and that, but there's no more trail. Jesse grows anxious, reacting to my indecision. She tries to lure me back the way we came.

I tell her we're not doing that. She responds with whimpers, dancing back and forth. That sets me off. "Hey, I'm the one calling the shots here," I growl at her. Then I ponder my next move. There's only one thing to do, really. I shoot a compass bearing due north. If there's a woods road running east/west, as shown on my map, we'll soon run into it. "Let's go!" I shout with all the authority I can muster, pressing into the trackless forest. Jesse follows obediently.

We bushwhack less than a hundred yards before stepping onto the sketchy woods road. Jesse gives me that I-wasn't-really-worried look. Yeah, right. Turning eastward, we soon stumble into an old, rusty signpost half-hidden by brush. It points in the general direction of Lost Pond. I drop my pack at the base of the sign and tramp down an overgrown trail until I reach the feeder stream where I'd been standing fifteen minutes earlier. Now it all makes sense. Back at the rusty sign, I whip out my map to finish orienting myself. Then I sit down to eat something. Lunch is a simple affair: trail mix, some crackers, beef jerky. Jesse gets a couple biscuits and we're both happy.

Slowly meandering eastward along the woods road, it's clear that no one has traveled this way in a long, long time. Fallen trees block the track every thirty or forty yards. Saplings grow waist high in the middle of the road. The trail underfoot is a deer path now, weaving through thickening brush. Every once in a while, I spot a snowmobile trail marker. That convinces me that this track could be opened again someday. But right now, it's forgotten.

Mid-afternoon. After daydreaming along the abandoned woods road for an hour or so, I spot an opening through the trees to my left. Can it be? Sure enough, there's a beaver pond fifty yards south of the woods road, about a hundred feet below us. It's small, deep and still. No brush around it. What a beauty! I drop my pack and take a long break to admire the gem before me.

Being a backwoods fisherman, I love little surprises like this. Located at the head of a mountain stream that eventually pours into Cedar River, this pond could be holding trout. If so, I could be the first person to fish it. Looks like there's good access to its deepest water, just above the dam. Hmm. Should I keep going until I reach Little Moose Lake or stay here for the night and fish the pond at dusk? Could be brook trout heaven. I've stumbled into beaver ponds like this before and pulled nine-inchers from them all day long. Or it could be a dud. What day is this? Thursday. That means I still have enough food for three or four more days. Why not stay a while?

Late afternoon, early evening. I've set up camp in the middle of the woods road, much to the dismay of any deer that might come along tonight. A flat, roomy spot surrounded by hardwoods, it feels like home immediately after I pitch the tarp and fashion a fire circle. The pond is in clear view. A beaver swims about the pond as I gather wood. Unhappy about me and Jesse being here, he slaps his tail against the water. Jesse is startled by it. We walk down to the pond's edge to fill a water bladder a bit later. The beaver slaps his tail one more time as he dives for cover.

Using my camp stove, I boil up brackish water to purify it. Don't trust my filter to do the job. The process goes quickly enough. Afterward, dinner is an expedient affair – more for Jesse's benefit than mine. I eat whatever doesn't need to be cooked. Jesse's bowl is the only thing that requires washing. Soon enough, dinner's over and camp is all squared away. With an hour or two of daylight left, I grab my rod and whistle for Jesse to follow me. She's surprised by this, thinking that we've settled in for the night. But she's on her feet in a heartbeat.

Reaching that patch of open ground next to the beaver dam is harder than I thought it would be. A thick stand of black spruce blocks direct access, so I'm forced to sweep widely to the left, through a small wet meadow just below the pond. Naturally, the meadow is crisscrossed by beaver channels, in anticipation of even newer ponds. I skip across a fallen log stretching over the largest channel. Jesse follows but her unsteady hind legs slip away beneath her, putting her chest-deep in muck for the second time today. She yelps, unable to escape the muck. I reach over and grab her by the fur to man-haul her free. Shaken by this, she follows me to the open ground with some reluctance. I coax her into a nice soft spot next to the pond to rest. She lies down with a heavy sigh.

Clouds of mayflies hatch shortly after the sun sinks into the trees. No fish rise but it's a glorious thing to behold such a strong hatch. I cast my artificial fly among the living ones, projecting myself into the rhythm of things. This profusion of aquatic life, far away from the hubbub of humanity, queues me to a cycle that's been turning for eons. My thoughts swim in the wonder and mystery of it all. Now I'm fishing more for perspective than anything else. Mesmerized by the silence and stillness of the pond, I stop waving my rod and simply watch things unfold around me. Eventually, a dragonfly buzzes my head, drawing me out of my reverie. Daylight has become twilight already. Better get back to camp.

After a quick wash in the brackish pond, I declare Jesse clean again. Then we head out. I fight my way through the dense spruce – hard going for me but easy on my four-legged companion who's low to the ground. A few cuts and scrapes later, I pop into the roomy hardwoods and scramble uphill. Jesse collapses into a clump of grass as soon as we reach camp. She's completely spent. It's been a long, rough day for her. I rub her neck, promising that tomorrow will be easier. She doesn't respond. Darkness comes fast. I strike a match, then hold it to the strips of birch bark piled inside the fire circle. Time for a little campfire meditation.

5

A small fire burns brightly in the circle of rocks before me. Its cheery orange flames provide good company as darkness descends. I've been here before – on my own in wild country with only a rough idea where I am. As always, the accompanying emotions are both oppressive and liberating. It's always a bit burdensome to be completely alone with one's thoughts in deep woods. But never is my head more clear than at times like these.

Jesse moves away from the fire, taking up guard duty at the edge of camp. With her back to me, she watches and listens for any kind of activity. A small creature rustles across the forest floor; a larger one bangs around the meadow below the beaver pond; mosquitoes whine. That's all that I can hear, anyhow, above the crackle of the campfire. The rest is deep forest silence, which torments ears accustomed to hearing so much more. Without realizing it at first, my mind invents cricket sounds to fill the void. Does Jesse do the same or is she more in tune with reality? I hear a slight humming sound in the distance, or at least *think* I hear something like that. It's the collective buzz of civilization, the dull echo of distant machinery. Or perhaps it's nothing at all.

Patches of deep blue sky filter through a web of branches directly overhead – the last glimmer of daylight. A green stick hisses then snaps loudly in the campfire. A wood thrush sings its melodious, flutelike song, reminding me of another place and time. Suddenly I'm twenty-four years old again, taking lunch somewhere in Oregon's Cascade Mountains. I remember a thrush landing on a tree branch not six feet away, serenading me. Never before had I ventured so deep into such a large wilderness area. Never before had I heard anything so beautiful. Later on that day, I left the beaten path in search of true wilderness. Twenty-odd years later, here I am doing much the same. What began as an impulse has become a lifelong habit.

Lost Pond was something of a disappointment. It wasn't the clearwater haven I'd hoped it would be. But this camp next to a relatively new beaver pond is a good consolation prize. So it goes when you leave the beaten path. Roll with the punches; be ready to be surprised. That's what I like most about backcountry travel, I suppose. It forces me to be flexible, to abandon my linear way of thinking. It forces me to deal more directly with the world. It makes my thoughts less abstract; my heart more receptive to *otherness*. But all these years of wandering and wondering – to what end? Today I've danced the spirit of the wild, no doubt about that. But am I any wiser for it? The wood thrush sings its forest hymn one last time this evening. I hear the earth rejoicing in that song, yet never have I felt such profound sadness. Perhaps this is only the passage of time leaving its mark on me. Or maybe I'm just tired. The fire dwindles until a skeleton of charred sticks collapses into a heap of glowing embers. I snuff out the remnants then go to bed.

First light. I awaken to the sound of breaking branches down by the beaver pond. Jesse hears it, too. A moment ago, I was playing with my grandkids in the land of dreams. Now I listen intently for the distinct rustle of deer moving swiftly through the forest. There it is! Then silence. A wood thrush sings loud and clear. Perhaps it's the same one that I heard last night. It reminds me of something Henry David Thoreau once wrote: "The thrush alone declares the immortal wealth and vigor that is in the forest..." That puts a smile on my face as I crawl from bed. But Thoreau isn't my guru – not any more. He never was, really. Guys like me don't have gurus. We have only an insatiable appetite for knowledge and the company of furry companions on hair-shirt adventures. Yeah, I've read Henry's journals. And I know enough about the man to know the limits of his vision. So to hell with him and gurus in general. As both a woods wanderer and wonderer, I'm on my own now. I always have been, really. Just me and wild nature… and my ever-present dog, who's reminding me that it's time to drop the food bag and get the day going.

While fixing breakfast, I can't help but laugh. Henry would have approved of my fierce individualism, wouldn't he? Yeah, marching to the beat of a different drummer and all that. I say "To hell with you, Henry," and he responds with ghostly applause. Ironic, really. By dismissing that 19th Century iconoclast, I embrace him.

Just then it all makes sense: the funk, my writer's angst, my being here in deep woods, last night's dream, everything. Each life is but a lens – just one more way of seeing things. It's not about me. It's about whatever bit of insight I can contribute to humankind's ongoing spiritual adventure. Someday my perspective might be of use to others, perhaps to my grandchildren or my great grandchildren. *Someone* has to point the way to the wild – why not me? I brood that no one cares about what I scribble down, but how the hell do I know what'll resonate with people a hundred years from now? It's not about me, that's the main thing. I'm just a tool that wild nature uses. I'm just a set of ears to hear the wood thrush's song, and a pen to record it. That's all.

Where to begin? How does one speak for the wild? A single tear burns down my cheek as I look around me at the unspeakable beauty and power of the surrounding forest, feeling the presence of God as the sun rises slowly over the silent pond. There are no words for it, really. The wild is its own reason for being. It has its own agenda. So does Jesse. She comes over to drool all over me, wondering what the holdup is. "I'm getting to it," I grumble, pushing her away. Now then... Where'd I put her pills?

"C'mon, Jes!" I shout after shouldering my pack, tramping eastward along the overgrown woods road. She sprints ahead of me in a sudden burst of energy. It's a brand new day and we're both feeling frisky. Temps in the 60s and nothing but blue sky overhead. It's a great day to be in the woods.

We follow a set of fresh deer tracks through a small wetland, then bear left as the narrow trail underfoot sweeps around Manbury Mountain. We're headed for Little Moose Lake, which I hope isn't overrun with people. According to my map, there's an unimproved dirt road skirting the northern rim of that lake. But my map is probably ten years old. The lake could be a resort by now. Or the road around it might be as forgotten as the trace I'm following. Won't know until I get there. Will reach it before noon. Hmm... With that thought, I cut my pace. No sense in racing out of the woods.

Eureka! I thought there might be a rivulet or two running off the mountain and sure enough, here's a nice one. The abandoned woods road crosses a stream small enough to jump across. Jesse immediately laps up the cold clear water. I drop my pack and extract a water filter from it. Then I fill both my bottles while sitting cross-legged on a patch of cool moss next to the stream. Mosquitoes hover over the nearby pool, more interested in seeking shelter from the rising heat than extracting blood from me. Jesse wades into another pool. I take advantage of the situation and wash her off a bit more. Then I splash cold water into my face. Didn't realize what a hardship last night's relatively dry camp was until now. Eighteen hours without running water – totally uncalled for.

The hike becomes a meander. No rush at all. Just beyond two posts where a gate once stood, the woods road becomes even harder to follow, splintering into divergent paths at overgrown logging yards. "Private Land" a sign warns in the middle of nowhere. I bear right as the trail forks one last time, choosing the path that veers downhill. I check my compass but it's all guesswork now. Reading the contours, I surmise that Little Moose Lake should crop up soon. A sketchy path quickly becomes a worn jeep trail entering bottomland thick with alders and willows. And sure enough, the lake pops into view as I cross the small wooden bridge over its outlet stream. To my great surprise, there's a cabin on a rocky outcrop about halfway up the lake. There's also a dirt road on the other side of the bridge. It's narrow but well maintained. And thus my excursion into deep woods ends, just like that.

6

Turning right onto the improved dirt road, I commence a long walk eastward. Presumably, the road follows the northern shoreline of Little Moose Lake, but there's no lake in sight and the unbroken row of "No Trespassing" signs nailed to trees on my right prevents me from going through the trees for a quick look. The owner of that cabin jealously guards his/her privacy. Whatever. The sooner I get back into the woods, the better.

The hot, midday sun burns directly overhead as Jesse and I tramp down the exposed corridor. The dusty road is awash in eye-squinting light. We take a water break in the shade once we're beyond the inhospitable signs, but are soon back on the move and puffing again.

My map shows a jeep track extending southward from the road a quarter mile to the northeastern corner of the lake. In my mind's eye, there's a primitive boat-launch at the end of that track with a nice place to camp nearby. Turning right onto a partially overgrown track, I pursue this daydream, hoping to reach the lake. No such luck. The track underfoot diminishes to a game trail on the other side of a small meadow, then slowly fades into open woods. Both Jesse and I sense that we're getting closer to water as the terrain slopes gently downward, but we turn around after ten minutes of bushwhacking. Once again, there seems to be a discrepancy between my map and reality.

Back on the dirt road, I soon hear a trickle of running water. A quick thrash through some high grass reveals a rivulet small enough to step across. Finding cool, clear water in a foot-deep pool, I drop my pack and pump both water bottles full. Jesse drinks her fill, of course. Then we're back on the dusty road again, headed southeast. When the road turns sharply north, I spot a rusty yellow gate blocking a woods road pointing due east. Hmm. Is this the track heading back to the Northville/Lake Placid Trail? After checking my compass, I start down it.

Once again, deer tracks thread through chest-high brush, weaving back and forth along the remnants of a woods road, dodging blowdown. It's the mere suggestion of a trail. After crossing a stream, I'm convinced that I'm going the right way. If things go well, I'll soon be standing on a bona fide trail again. Worse case scenario, the track underfoot will drop into that wetland barely visible through the trees to the south. If that happens, I'll keep to high ground.

Jesse gets all excited when finally we step back onto the Northville/Lake Placid Trail, thus completing our sixteen-mile loop. After sniffing around a bit, she smiles. So do I. For the first time since yesterday morning, I know *exactly* where I am. Quick lunch break, then we head north along the well-beaten path. The hike is so easy that I'm soon paying more attention to wildflowers than anything else. Indian pipe, closed gentian and white wood asters line the trail. It's late summer in the North Woods. Soon the fringes of hobblebush leaves will rust and a hint of autumn will be in the air.

A half-hour of steady hiking is all it takes to reach a high-use campsite on the reedy shores of Cedar Flow. Jesse knows that the truck is parked a mile and a half farther north, so she's surprised when I start setting up camp. She thinks our trek is over, but I'm not ready to go home just yet. Why not stay here a day or two?

Puttering around camp like an old man, it's late evening before I have everything squared away: tarp pitched, wood gathered, food bag slung and Jesse cleaned up. I spend an inordinate amount of time picking up trash and tidying up the fire pit. Dinner is an expedient affair – a dehydrated meal and a few handfuls of trail mix. At dusk I build a bigger fire than necessary, burning up charred pieces of wood scattered about the area. Jesse goes to bed early.

Morning, day six. A woodpecker is hard at work directly overhead; a loon calls from the waterway. I slept well last night despite a midnight chill. The sun is high in the sky over Cedar Flow before I commence my breakfast ritual. Must've been more tired than I thought. Jesse looks exhausted. Good thing we're not going anywhere today.

    After Jesse devours her breakfast, I give her a second helping. I do not do this lightly. It cuts into our limited food supply, meaning that we'll have to leave the woods tomorrow. But this trip's over for the most part. I have several blisters on my feet and Jesse is at the limit of. her endurance. I've pushed her long enough.

    A steady stream of hikers tramp up and down the nearby trail. A few stop to chat while I putter around camp doing a lot of nothing. One thru-hiker shows off a homemade stove. A father/son team takes a much-needed break, trading stories with me. But most of the day it's just me and Jesse along the shores of Cedar Flow, watching a golden eagle soaring over the water, listening to loons, taking in the expansive view.

    Early evening, I join a blue heron wading amid the reeds, fishing for dace. Standing thigh-deep in water, I catch and release a dozen of those tiny fish. It's a goofy pleasure, tossing my fly among live ones only to have baitfish suck it down. I don't care. The subtle change of evening light and the sensation of mud oozing between my toes is reason enough to stand here. Jesse watches from a comfy tuft of grass on the edge of shore, drifting in an out of consciousness. She couldn't look any more content.

At dusk Jesse goes crazy on me, pacing back and forth along the trail as I start a fire. She's had enough of the wild and wants to leave right now. I tell her we'll hike out tomorrow, but she's not listening. Twice she disappears from view, heading down the trail on her own. I end up tying her to a tree in the middle of camp. Catching her silhouette in the campfire light a bit later on, I can see how uneasy she is. Rowdy young men camped a half mile south are making a lot of noise. Maybe that's what's bothering her. I unleash her and she clings to my side. I cut my fire gazing short, knowing that Jesse wants to settle in for the night. It has come to this.

Down by the water, cleaning up before going to bed, I gaze up at the Milky Way stretching across the black canopy. I marvel at the immensity of space and our place in it. I sit on a rock for a while, drawing Jesse closer. A shooting star streaks across the night sky. Another one follows a short while later. I try to make a wish but nothing comes to mind. I rub my dog behind the ears, instead. What was it that had me so bent out of shape a week ago? It doesn't matter any more.

Sunday, seventh day out here. Leaving wild country is always tough when foul weather isn't nipping at your heels. Today couldn't be more pleasant, with temps in the 60s and plenty of sunshine brightening the forest. I linger in camp as long as possible but am back on the trail by late morning. The hike goes fast. We're out of the woods before noon. I wipe a week's worth of cobwebs away from my truck before firing it up. Jesse is all smiles as she sits on the passenger's side, head out the window. A couple miles down the road, I stick my head out the window, as well, for a taste of breezy happiness. Yeah, it has come to this: the needs and desires of man and dog blurring. For the past five and a half years, Jesse has been my guru, helping me wrestle all my abstractions into perspective. She's been a good companion in that regard. But we've just finished our last big outing together and it won't be long before I have to put her down. It'll be hard returning to the woods without her.

About the Author

Walt McLaughlin received a degree in philosophy from Ohio University in 1977 and has been wondering, wandering and writing ever since. He has over a dozen books in print, including a narrative about his immersion in the Alaskan bush, *Arguing with the Wind*, and one about backpacking through the Adirondacks, *The Allure of Deep Woods*. He is also the force behind a small press called Wood Thrush Books, and has selected and published the works of several 19th Century writers including *The Laws of Nature: Excerpts from the Writings of Ralph Waldo Emerson*. He lives in Swanton, Vermont with his wife, Judy.

For more information about Walt's books, visit the WTB website: **www.woodthrushbooks.com**

Go to **www.facebook.com\WaltMcLaughlin** to check out his Facebook page, or read his regularly posted blogs at **www.woodswanderer.com**

www.ingramcontent.com/pod-product-compliance
Lightning Source LLC
Chambersburg PA
CBHW030019290326
41934CB00005B/400

9 7 8 1 7 3 4 5 1 7 5 2 1